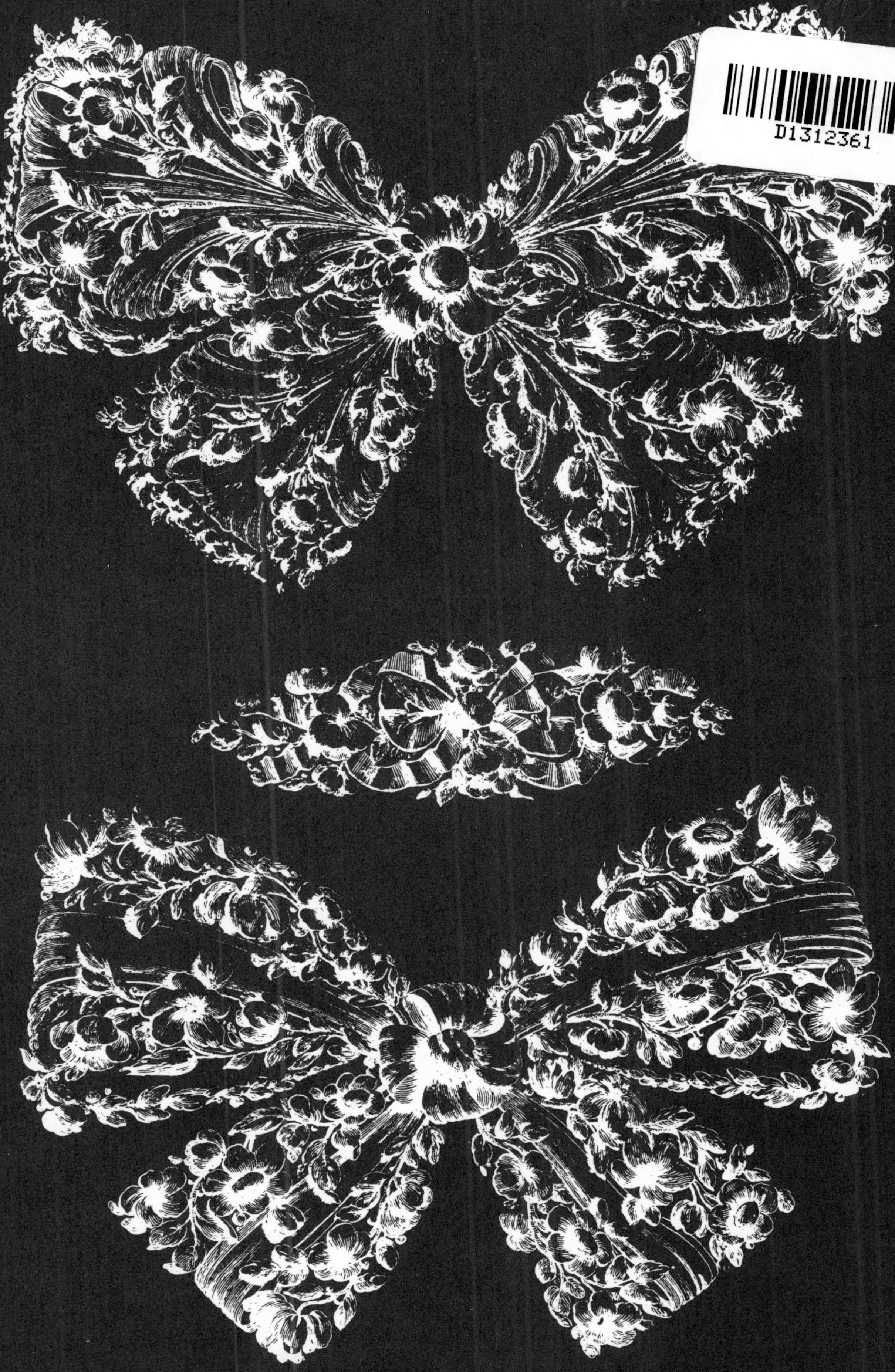

Jewelry

THE SMITHSONIAN ILLUSTRATED LIBRARY OF ANTIQUES

General Editor: Brenda Gilchrist

Jewelry

Marie-Louise d'Otrange Mastai

COOPER-HEWITT MUSEUM

The Smithsonian Institution's National Museum of Design

ENDPAPERS

Eighteenth-century design for a brooch. European. Picture Collection, Cooper-Hewitt Museum Library

FRONTISPIECE

All passing moods and fashions of the nineteenth century were faithfully reflected in bracelets. *Clockwise from upper left*: An articulated solid-gold cuff bracelet with six frames set with an oval garnet and topped with a bow of black enamel, French; a hinged gold bangle with a scroll motif of *pavé* turquoises and pearls, gold chains and tassels, American; a gilt-metal clasp bracelet with motifs of double (or twin) trefoils forming the nine links of the band and framing the large aquamarine, German; a hinged solid-gold bangle in the shape of a ribbon band with enameled plaid pattern, French. Cooper-Hewitt Museum, all given from the Estate of and in memory of Mrs. Robert B. Noyes, except clasp bracelet, bequest of Mrs. John Innes Kane

To my long-suffering husband, Boleslaw Mastai

Printed in the United States of America
Library of Congress Catalog Card Number: 78-62730

Art Direction, Design: Joseph B. Del Valle

Picture Editor: Lisa Little

Contents

Colorplate 1

1 Introduction

The world of antique jewelry fascinates collectors and scholars alike. Whether a priceless creation or a modest pin, a piece of antique jewelry has meaning and interest for the historian, anthropologist, art student, geologist and antiquarian. For in the long, colorful evolution of jewelry, virtually every human emotion, from the finest artistic impulses to greed, has been lavished on the creating and wearing of fine jewelry. Jewelry has by turns been regarded as symbol, as beautiful ornament, and as investment—or loot. It is true still that most of us are first fascinated by jewelry because of its aura of preciousness, since jewels are usually formed of valuable substances like gold, diamonds and pearls.

The line dividing fine art from less exalted examples is always tenuous and wavering, but never more so than when one seeks to distinguish between the work of the craftsman-jeweler and the artist-jeweler, or "jewelist," as I have tentatively entitled him. A term of this sort is needed to distinguish the true creator of jewels (whether he is responsible simply for the design or participates also in the making, as was usually the case during the great periods of jewelry as an art) from the merely competent craftsman. At present the term jeweler must still do for both, with qualifications necessary but also often omitted. As a result of such omission, few laymen realize, for instance, that while Benvenuto Cellini was indeed a jewelist—that is, both a designer and a craftsman—the renowned Russian court jeweler Peter Carl Fabergé was not. Fabergé's principal role was as an organizer of the multiple talents and skills of the men in his employ.

Many artists of the first magnitude—Leonardo, Dürer, Holbein the Younger, Botticelli, Ghirlandaio, to name but a few—actually designed jewelry. Others, like Rembrandt, are not known to have done so. Yet all were jewelists with their paintbrushes, depicting countless

Colorplate 1.
The famous azure blue Hope Diamond, believed to be one of the fragments into which the fabled Blue Diamond of the French crown jewels was cut after it was stolen from the royal treasury at the time of the French Revolution. The Hope Diamond's present setting was designed by Pierre Cartier in 1911. Smithsonian Institution, National Museum of Natural History, gift of Harry Winston

imaginary jewels in their paintings: one need only recall the golden jewels Rembrandt bestowed so lavishly on his biblical and mythological subjects, jewels never obtainable at the shop of any Amsterdam or Rotterdam goldsmith—or anywhere else on earth, for that matter.

The usual run of antique jewels of course falls far short of such magic, yet the conclusion to be drawn is evident. A collector of antique jewelry is first and foremost a collector of art. The collector may have other interests as well—antiquarian, historical, technical—but a concern for jewelry as art is the basis of proper understanding and appreciation.

On the practical plane, it is a mistake to equate the terms jewel and gem; they should not be confused. A jewel is an object made by man, whereas a gem, though it may have been polished or faceted by hand, is a natural substance, commonly a mineral. It is true that in our day chemists can create a synthetic diamond, ruby or sapphire, and these stones are thus man-made. However, they still do not become jewels until mounted as articles of personal adornment.

The difference between a gem and a jewel is illustrated by one of the most celebrated gems of all time, the Hope Diamond (colorplate 1). It is said to have come from a huge blue diamond that was mined in India some three centuries ago and was brought to Europe by the seventeenth-century French merchant-traveler Jean-Baptiste Tavernier. This original stone, which was sold to Louis XIV of France and became known as the Blue Diamond, was transformed by the skill of the diamond cutter into a magnificent faceted gem subsequently stolen during the French Revolution. The Blue Diamond has never been recovered, but the Hope is thought to be a fragment cut from it. In its present incarnation, the famous stone has been set in an utterly simple mount: an unadorned circlet of diamonds, allowing the extraordinary size and coloristic beauty of the stone to be appreciated to the full. This is implied in its present title of "Hope Diamond" rather than "Hope Jewel," as it might be called if its chief merit derived instead from extraneous contributions of design and craftsmanship.

In troubled times the same fate—resetting—has befallen even jewels adorned with gems of much less value. On occasion, of course, jewels have been broken up not by thieves but by their rightful owners, who wanted the gems reset in a more fashionable mode or needed to convert them into cash. As a result of such hazards, precious antique jewelry is comparatively rare, particularly jewelry of the eighteenth and nineteenth centuries, when the use of gems in stylized patterns became very popular, causing much resetting of older-style jewelry.

In earlier periods, before jewels were commonly set with gems, craftsmen had been able to produce objects of extraordinary beauty

1.
The preciousness of a jewel is not always gauged in carats. With champlevé enameling its only ornamentation, this medieval gilt-copper armlet fetched more than two million dollars at auction in 1978. One of a pair believed to have been made for the Holy Roman Emperor Frederick I Barbarossa, the piece is of outstanding historical interest as well as of great artistic merit and the utmost rarity. The superb multicolor enameling depicts the Crucifixion. (The companion piece, depicting the Resurrection, is in the Louvre.) Detail. Rhenish or Mosan, twelfth century. Germanisches Nationalmuseum, Nuremberg

merely using gold and enamel. Today, these pieces are properly appreciated. In 1978, for example, an enameled arm ornament dating from the twelfth century was sold at auction in London for more than two million dollars, although the value of the basic materials involved is relatively negligible (plate 1). There can be little doubt that had this armlet been encrusted with gems instead of the few flakes of enamel that satisfied the anonymous artist who here created a masterpiece, it would not have escaped the despoilers and survived the intervening eight centuries.

Fascination with gems is deeply rooted in human consciousness. As far back as the Bronze Age, rough garnets were pierced and strung to form objects designed for personal adornment. Yet even this represents only a later phase in the development of jewelry. For the earliest, we must go back to the very dawn of prehistory and visualize one of our primitive ancestors stooping to pick up some shiny pebble or gleaming polished shell that attracted his fancy. Next, he might have wished to keep the admired trinket and carry it about with him, and so secreted it in the folds of his fur garment or tucked it into his thickly matted hair. Eventually, he might have evolved some contraption of braided reed or grass—possibly a small pouch—in which to hang the trinket on a cord around his neck. This is all hypothetical, but it may well be the way in which the first "gem" and then the first "jewel" came into existence.

Perhaps in due course this predecessor of the Hope Diamond attracted attention, respect or envy, thus bringing to its owner a measure of prestige and power. Jewels have indeed traditionally served as symbols of dignity and of rank as well as of wealth. They have served, too, as manifestations of religious belief, of allegiance to a sovereign or cause, of devotion to a lover. They have even played a utilitarian role. Egyptian signet rings, for example, were probably functional in origin, in that they were devised to carry seals, or signets, carved with ideographs. In the highly sophisticated society of the Renaissance, a lowly whistle could be raised to the status of a jewel, though admittedly it was designed by no less an artist than Dürer (plate 52, see page 71). The earliest watches, dating from the sixteenth century, were as much decorative objects or portable bibelots as timepieces, and later watches would dangle at a lady's waist together with various lilliputian household articles as part of the romantic chatelaine beloved by our great-great-grandmothers.

But these roles of jewelry are auxiliary. Our prehistoric "jewel" was surely the result of man's first dim but growing awareness of the harmony of color, line and form, and the exquisite jewels produced in later times have been a response to much the same awareness, if on a different scale. The impulse toward creating jewelry is in fact not so far removed from that which has led man to raise vast monuments, create heroic statuary or paint huge murals. Indeed, jewelry is not always small, particularly jewelry with royal or imperial associations. Crowns, starting with the cumbrous, miterlike double crown of Egypt, have often been crushing burdens for the wearers, and even commonplace court jewels, if one may call them that, are frequently very large. The splendid stomacher (plate 73, see page 91) worn by Queen Charlotte of England when she posed for a state portrait must have been almost as weighty as a knight's armor; heavily gem-encrusted, it extends from the bosom to well below the waist.

Particularly massive pieces of jewelry, however, are not always unreasonably large. On ecclesiastical garments, even so imposing an object as the ancient cope morse shown in colorplate 14 (see page 63) would seem fittingly proportioned. Size in this instance also had the happy side effect of providing the anonymous Gothic artist-craftsman with additional scope for a brilliant display of talent as a sculptor. The wonderfully modeled figures are hardly smaller—or less well-crafted—than some of the famed Tanagra statuettes of ancient Greece. No one would dream of calling these "applied" or "decorative" art, as all too often is done with jewelry.

It is true that because of the inflexibility of the materials employed, jewelry has seldom been the medium in which an artistic creation is conceived. One cannot, after all, jot down a sudden inspiration on onyx or sketch it in molten gold. But the same limitations apply to sculptural works on a grand scale. Let us not forget that Michelangelo's Titans did not begin as works in marble but as thumbnail sketches.

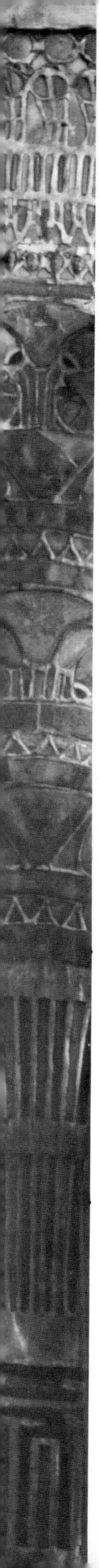

2 The Age of Gold

The period extending from the beginning of recorded history to the eve of the Christian Era covers approximately thirty-five hundred years. Scholars in various fields have approached it from many points of view. For the collector of antique jewelry, it may simply be classified as the Age of Gold (not to be confused with the Golden Age of peace and prosperity sung by Greek and Roman poets). The sense is strictly literal: the period was remarkable for the gold objects and decorations of every kind produced in lands bordering the Mediterranean. The art of the goldsmith girdled the midland sea with a glittering zone, and many of the lustrous artifacts still survive to bear witness to the splendors of these vanished Mediterranean civilizations.

Egypt, not surprisingly, leads the way, being among the first in time and second to none in achievement. Indeed, in our day, Egypt is as renowned for her ancient jewels as for her pyramids. This is due chiefly to the discovery in 1922 of the treasure-laden tomb of a young ruler of the Eighteenth Dynasty, Tutankhamun (reigned c. 1334–1325 B.C.). The name of this pharaoh has become a household word, and his treasures have been made famous the world over through exhibits and reproductions. But while the jewels of Tutankhamun are undoubted masterworks of Egyptian art, it should be remembered

2.
Tutankhamun and his consort, as depicted on the inner back panel of a throne found in the young pharaoh's tomb. Besides their elaborate crowns, the couple's attire includes coiflike imbricated wigs, broad collars, cuff bracelets and girdles adorned with gold. On the table behind the queen is another broad collar. Egyptian, c. 1334–1325 B.C. Egyptian Museum, Cairo

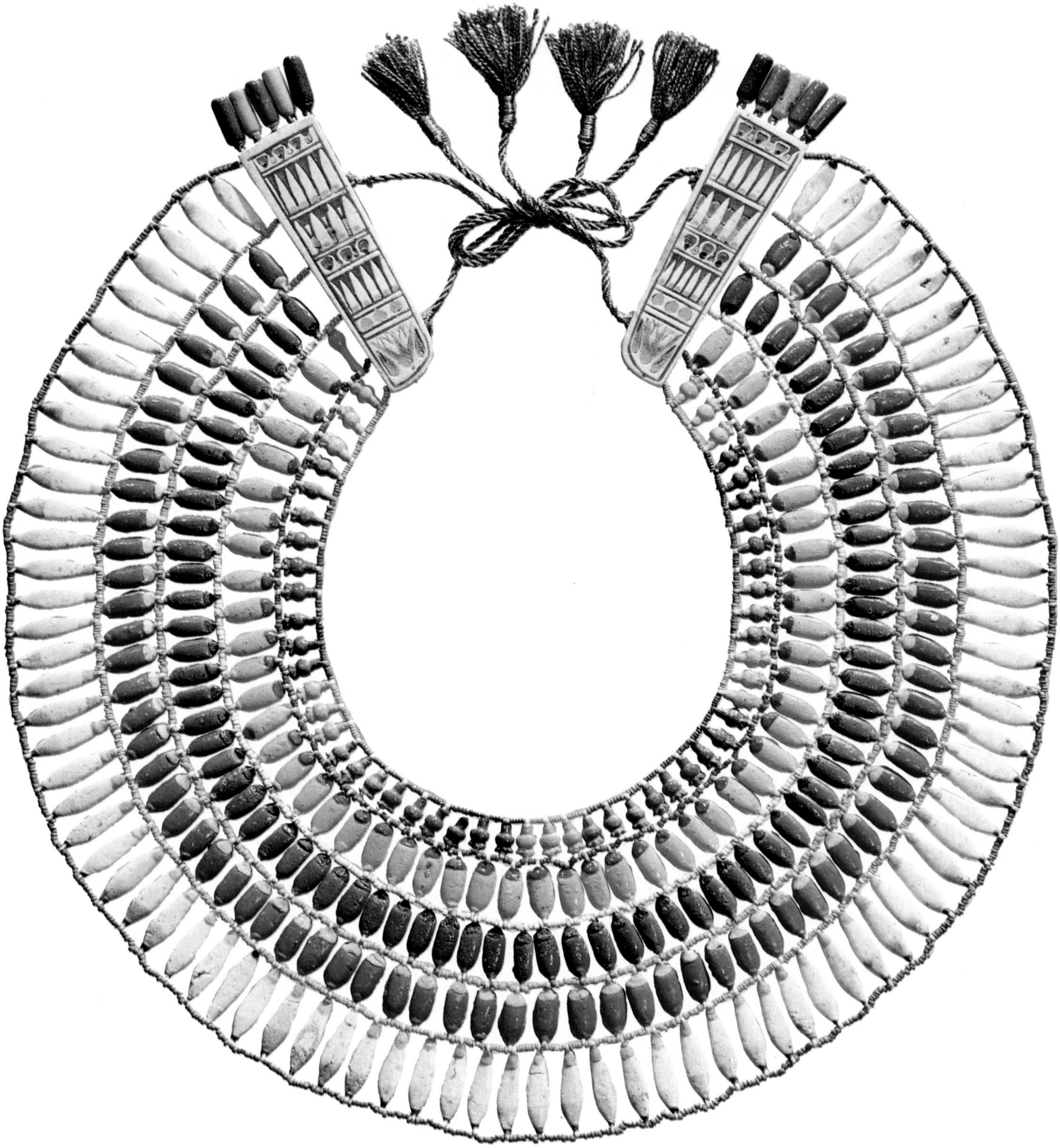

that they date from the era Egyptologists call the New Kingdom (c. 1570–1085 B.C.)—that is, the midpoint of ancient Egyptian history.

This means that Tutankhamun's treasures stand midway in the record of Egyptian jewelry. The earliest examples, produced perhaps a score of centuries before, were simple and artless, consisting mainly of strings of beads of shell, stone or baked clay, eventually with a coating of vitreous blue glaze (we may note in passing that this blue would continue as a major color in Egyptian ornamentation). About 2600 B.C., during the earliest dynasties of the Old Kingdom, goldsmithing made its appearance; and although its first efforts were modest, they cannot be called primitive, for they are marked by precisely the sobriety now prized in the best of modern jewelry.

After another thousand years had passed, but still well before the reign of Tutankhamun, the essentials of Egyptian design and craftsmanship had been established. Following Tutankhamun, textures and color schemes would remain basically the same for another millennium, although increasing use would be made of such semiprecious substances as lapis lazuli, turquoise, amethyst, carnelian, obsidian and quartz—a use carried at times, as with some of the Tutankhamun jewels, to excess. The processes involved the entire repertory of the goldsmith and jeweler, except that there was no faceting of gems. Gilding with exceedingly thin leaves of beaten gold was practiced with great skill, and the techniques of *granulation* and *filigree* were employed, though sparingly. The Egyptian jeweler, like his counterparts in other fields of Egyptian dynastic art, retained above all a preference for the pure, uncluttered line.

Since jewelry is usually intended to adorn parts of the human anatomy, clad or unclad, the types of jewelry used in Egypt are still in use: necklaces, bracelets, armlets, anklets, rings, girdles, combs, diadems. In certain respects, however, Egyptian jewels were specifically suited to the Egyptian climate, costume and customs. A favorite was the *broad collar*, a wide band made of tiered beads or other ornaments, which showed to great advantage on bare shoulders or on the sheer pleated fabric of a garment (plate 2). This ornament is so familiar to us from wall paintings and statuary that we can hardly picture an inhabitant of ancient Egypt, male or female, without it, and indeed it seems to have been worn by the humblest as well as the highest, except perhaps for laborers engaged in heavy work. The elements used varied widely in value. Some broad collars were fashioned of gold; in the earliest dynasties the pharaohs often gave these as awards. Others were made of brightly colored faience symbolizing such natural elements as palm leaves, flowers or berries, grapes or dates (colorplate 2). The flower collars were stylized echoes of their prototype, for pieces made of actual blooms have been preserved. One is at the Metropolitan Museum of Art in New York City; another may still be seen as it was thrown by a last mourner over the neck and shoulders

Colorplate 2.
A broad collar of faience beads. The stylized elements of the large, tiered necklace represent cornflowers, dates and lotus petals. For the Egyptians, broad collars such as this were as much wearing apparel as jewelry. (The tasseled cord is a modern restoration.) Egyptian, late Eighteenth Dynasty (c. 1570–1293 B.C.). Metropolitan Museum of Art, New York, Rogers Fund, 1940

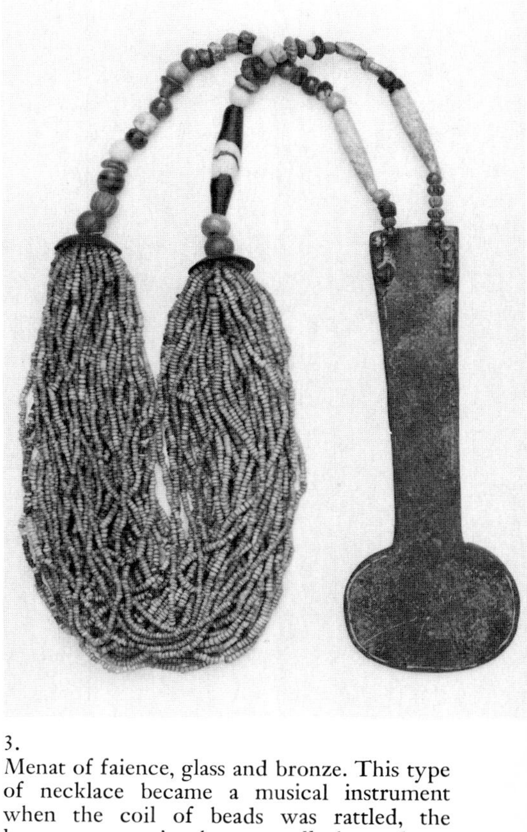

3.
Menat of faience, glass and bronze. This type of necklace became a musical instrument when the coil of beads was rattled, the large counterpoise that normally hung down the back serving as a handle. Egyptian, c. 1386–1349 B.C. Metropolitan Museum of Art, New York, museum excavations, 1911–12

of a lifelike polychrome wooden statue of "the overseer of works, Kha," now in his last resting place, the Egyptian Museum in Turin, Italy. Frail mementos of this sort are both touching and significant: they exemplify an awareness of nature as reflected in art—as does the repeated use in Egyptian jewelry of seashells, tiger teeth and scarabs, either stylized or actual.

Another uniquely Egyptian form of necklace is the *menat*, or *menyet*, which had a twofold function, serving as a musical instrument as well as an ornament (plate 3). Single pendants on a chain were not uncommon, but one (colorplate 3, bottom left) merits special attention because of the unique three-dimensional quality of the small pharoah figure and also because of the crouching posture, highly uncharacteristic of a god-king. Perhaps the realism here reflects the influence of the pharaoh Akhenaton (reigned c. 1350–1334 B.C.), predecessor of Tutankhamun, a mystic and royal rebel who attempted to revolutionize not only the religion of his land but its artistic vision as well. Akhenaton is said to have sought to instill a naturalistic element into Egyptian art in place of the hieratic stylization imposed by the ruling priestly caste.

Egyptian earrings were probably of Asian inspiration. They are frequently seen as large gold disks glimpsed amid a somber mass of hair in depictions of dancing girls. But this was not their only form, nor was their use restricted to women. It is believed that young princes also wore earrings, at least until they reached manhood. A remarkable pair of earrings with duck heads and falcon wings (colorplate 3, top left) was found in Tutankhamun's tomb and shows signs of actual wear; perhaps he himself wore them as a boy. The heads are made of blue glass, and the naturalistic treatment contrasts with the stylization of the wings. Blue, as indicated earlier, is ever in evidence in Egyptian jewelry. These earrings, as well as many pectorals and other jewels, display the inlay work so characteristic of Egyptian jewelry: stones or beads cemented into sections formed by metal strips.

Bracelets and armlets were generally of the cuff type, with wide bands of chased and engraved gold and a bas-relief effect (cuff bracelets can be seen in plate 2). Others might be built up, like miniature collars, of tiers of tubular or spherical beads bound at intervals in gold.

Wigs were worn by both men and women. As is the case today, they could be made of actual hair or of some fiber resembling hair. Women's wigs were typically shoulder length, constructed perhaps of numerous plaited strands interspersed with jewels. Other wigs resembled a cap or a veil and might be made of metallic mesh, aligned gold rosettes, overlapping scales or juxtaposed tubular beads. On the back of Tutankhamun's throne in plate 2, both the young pharaoh and his queen are shown wearing what appear to be wigs of the coif

Colorplate 3.

Top left: A pair of duck-head earrings from the tomb of Tutankhamun. Under the clear glass buttons on the studs are miniature portraits of the pharaoh that may be made of fused particles of colored glass. If so, it would be the earliest recorded instance of this very delicate technique of jewelry ornamentation. Gold with various inlays; duck heads of translucent blue glass.

Top right: A richly inlaid pectoral pendant from Tutankhamun's tomb, depicting the sun god Horus in the form of a falcon. The red disk on the bird's head represents the rising sun. The back of the pendant is of plain gold, with the bird's details chased in the surface. (The tasseled cord is a modern restoration.) Gold, lapis lazuli, turquoise, carnelian and light blue glass.

Bottom left: A solid gold pendant (suspension chain not shown) from Tutankhamun's tomb. This miniature effigy of a pharaoh (possibly Amenhotep III, but probably Tutankhamun) is rendered in a naturalistic style always rare in Egyptian art and startlingly unexpected in a jewel.

Bottom right: A pectoral plaque from Tutankhamun's tomb, with three distinct religious symbols: the *udjat* eye (or eye of Horus), flanked by the sacred uraeus at right and the vulture of the goddess Nekhbet at left. The smaller plaque is the counterpoise needed to keep the front pendant in place. Gold, precious stones and colored glass.

Egyptian, c. 1334–1325 B.C. Egyptian Museum, Cairo

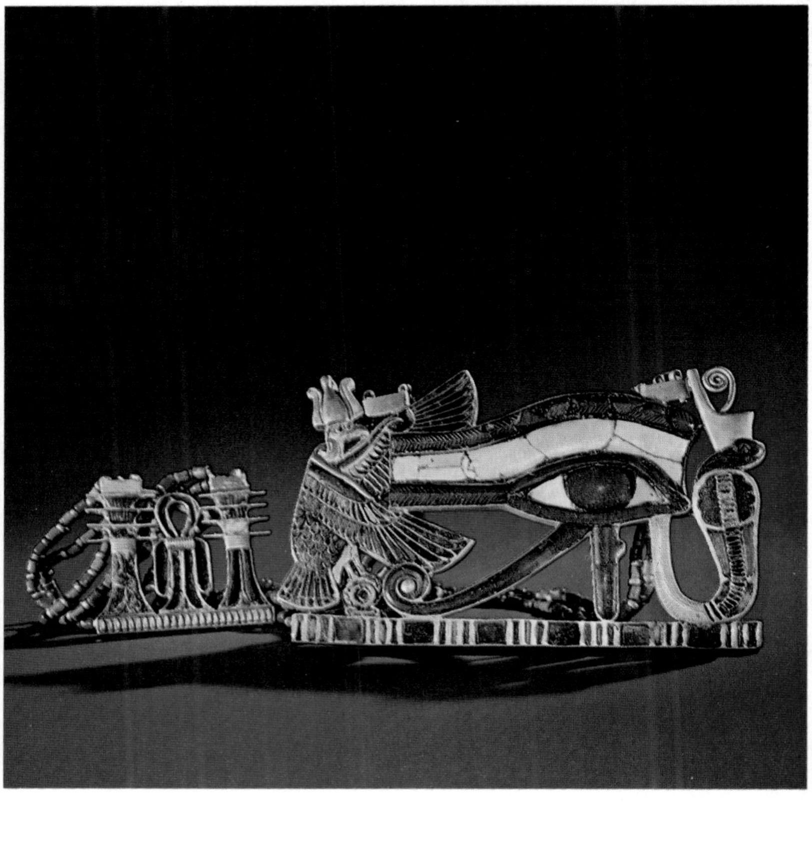

COLORPLATE 3

4.
A bronze statuette with gold hoops in the pierced ears, honoring Bastet, the Egyptian cat goddess. The incised collar of stylized lotus blossoms may have been painted or inlaid. Egyptian, c. 900–300 B.C. Metropolitan Museum of Art, New York, funds from various donors, 1958

Colorplate 4.
An exquisite necklace of precious drop and ball beads, with a trapezoidal pectoral pendant. Presented to Princess Sit-Hathor-Yunet by her royal father, Sesostris II (reigned c. 1897–1878 B.C.), it ranks as one of the supreme masterpieces of ancient Egyptian jewelry. Gold, carnelian, lapis lazuli, turquoise and green feldspar. Egyptian, Twelfth Dynasty (c. 2000–1786 B.C.). Metropolitan Museum of Art, New York, contribution from Henry Walters and the Rogers Fund, 1916

type, in a beautiful shade of blue, closely hugging the contours of their heads.

In this instance, the young couple's stylized wigs are topped by formal crowns of more than usual magnificence and beauty. If these are looked upon as jewelry—and they were certainly composed of precious substances—they would then have to be distinguished as pharaonic rather than simply Egyptian, since only the monarch and his kin would be entitled to wear them. The same restriction would of course apply to what are among the outstanding jewels in the Tutankhamun treasure: the several flails and crooks—encrusted with gold, faience and colored glass, and emblematic of Osiris—that were probably an Egyptian equivalent of such Western royal symbols as the orb and the scepter.

The famous gold mask worn by Tutankhamun in his third inner coffin should probably be ranked as a masterpiece of funerary jewelry—that is, jewelry expressly made to be buried with the dead for use after death—even though it is far richer and more substantial than funerary jewelry ordinarily is. After all, this mask was intended for a pharaoh, and was expected to be worn by the transfigured ruler not only through the long sleep in the tomb but also actively in his afterlife as the sun god.

Jewelry was associated with the worship of most of the gods and goddesses in the Egyptian pantheon, and their statues were lavished with such adornments as collars, earrings, necklaces and bracelets. A particularly beguiling example, made in homage to the cat-headed goddess Bastet, is a bronze statuette of a cat wearing gold earrings in its pierced ears (plate 4).

Necklaces with a large breast piece, or pectoral, afforded the Egyptian artist full scope for impressive compositions and, when bearing sacred symbols, were doubtless intended to protect the wearer from harm—as the reliquaries of the Christian faith were and are intended to do. The pectorals belonging to Tutankhamun include one depicting his tutelary deities, the vulture and the cobra, and another that represents the sun god Horus in the form of a falcon (see colorplate 3, top right). The falcon pectoral shows the divine bird with its wings outspread so as to form a half circle. The design itself is remarkable, but the pendant displays another, subtler refinement of the jeweler's art, for it has two rings under the top edge of each wing through which its tasseled cord could be slipped, thus avoiding the dangling effect that would result were the plaque hung, medal-like, from a single ring. The portions of the cord that run between the rings, however, were visible when the necklace was worn. In the vulture and cobra pectoral, the suspension rings were so placed that an even greater stability was achieved, and the problem of the cord was eliminated. Technical details like these were evidently carefully thought out by Egyptian jeweler-craftsmen and epitomized

a tradition handed down from generation to generation. The pectoral in colorplate 4, for example, dating back to a period well before Tutankhamun, belonged to a princess of the Twelfth Dynasty (c. 2000–1786 B.C.). It has most gracefully been made an integral part of the chain of drop and ball beads from which it depends. Thus this pectoral, too, is able to lie quite flat on the breast of the wearer.

The ingenuity of Egyptian master jewelers seems to have been equal to every challenge. It was they who evolved not only bracelets and necklaces but that most personal jewel: the signet ring (plate 5). Early examples consist of little more than a functional mount, stirrup-shaped, for a reversible carved seal, one side in the form of a scarab, the other engraved with hieroglyphs. Rings of this type may have been worn as pendants rather than on the finger. At any rate, Egyptian rings soon began to resemble the rings familiar to us: circular loops fitting the finger smoothly and closely, and with *bezels* of various shapes provided to secure an engraved seal or other valuable object.

Ancient Egypt, secure in her strength and wealth, was able to search for perfection. Other nations of the Levant and Near East, while also familiar with the goldsmith's craft at an early date, were wracked by warfare. It can be assumed that they produced less jewelry than Egypt, and also that much of what they did produce was lost as a result of foreign and domestic conflict. Nevertheless, excavation of royal tombs has uncovered a variety of artifacts, including jewels of unsurpassed virtuosity and originality. A Sumerian helmet of hammered electrum (plate 6), which resembles a flat, close-fitting metal wig, not only can hold its own next to the very finest craftsmanship Egypt then had to offer, but it also prefigures the towering achievements of Greek art. Another Sumerian head ornament of the same period (about 2500 B.C.), but this one for a woman's head, develops a floral theme with charming fantasy and great elegance. This lovely relic suggests tragedy as well: it was worn by one of the human sacrifices found in the death pits of Ur.

Indeed, the jewels of antiquity seem often to glisten as much with the dark glow of blood as with the brilliance of gold. Even the island of Crete, itself a jewel on the bosom of the sapphire blue Mediterranean, is darkly shadowed by such legends as that of the monstrous Minotaur. Yet we know that jewels of great charm and originality were created there. One of the most famous to have survived is a gold pendant representing two hornets facing each other, with bodies curved inward so as to touch at the tips of the abdomen, and wings extended horizontally. This is as masterful a work as any Egyptian entomic jewel, whether depicting the familiar scarab or the fly. A special kind of pectoral representing highly stylized flies was bestowed as an Egyptian military award; the hornet pendant may have served a similar purpose in Crete.

5.
Two Egyptian signet rings. *Top*: An early scarab ring on a "stirrup" mount that belonged to Princess Sit-Hathor-Yunet, daughter of the pharaoh Sesostris II. It probably was worn as a pendant. Gold inlay with carnelian, lapis lazuli and green feldspar. Twelfth Dynasty (c. 2000–1786 B.C.).

Bottom: A fully evolved signet finger ring of gold, with bezel and annular band completely united. Early Eighteenth Dynasty (c. 1570–1293 B.C.).

Metropolitan Museum of Art, New York, contribution from Henry Walters and the Rogers Fund, 1916 (scarab ring), and gift of Edward S. Harkness, 1926 (signet finger ring)

6.
Hammered from a single sheet of electrum (a natural alloy of gold and silver, pale yellow in color), this wiglike helmet once graced the head of a princely young denizen of ancient Ur. Sumerian, c. 2500 B.C. Iraq Museum, Baghdad

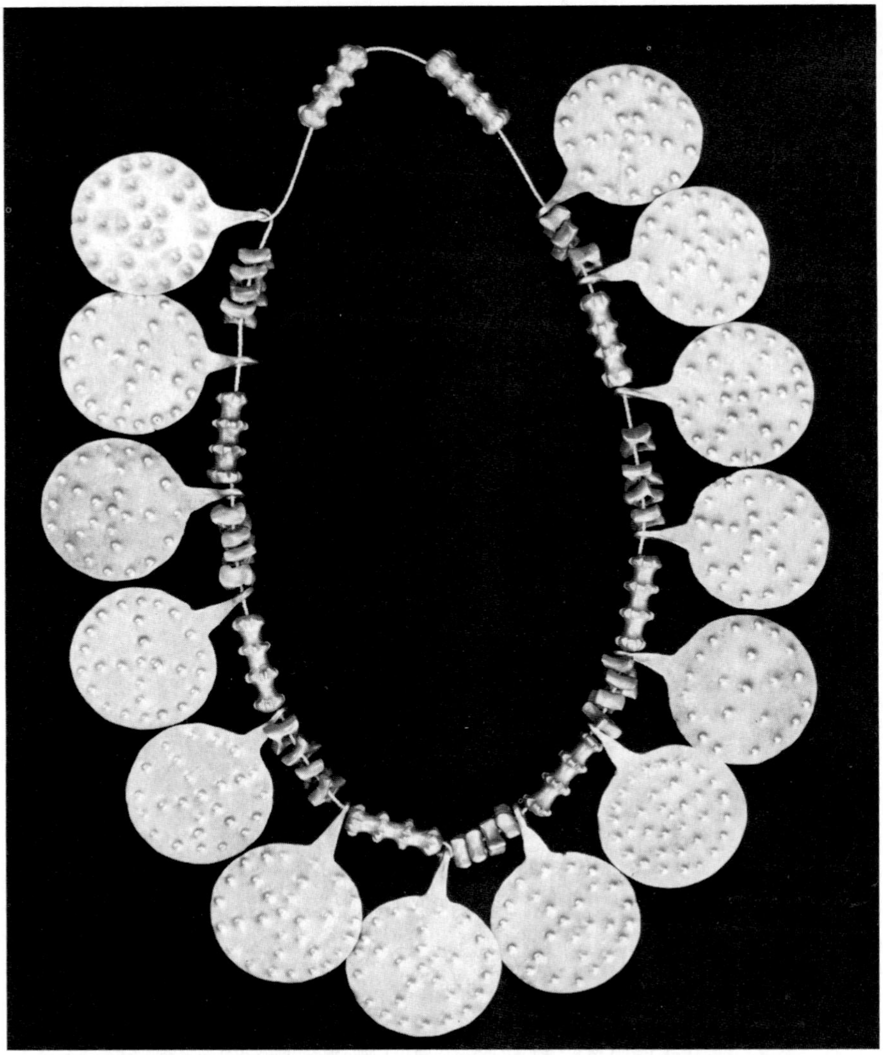

7

8

There was a good deal of cultural interchange in the ancient Mediterranean world, thanks especially to the Phoenicians, those tireless travelers and traders. Phoenician jewelry is thus, not unnaturally, highly eclectic, assimilating elements from other contemporary civilizations. The showcase, as it were, of Phoenician elegance is the famous bust of a noblewoman known as the Lady of Elche, after the city in Spain where it was discovered. The bust, now in the Louvre, is bedecked with a broad diadem, two large, wheel-like elements that encase the face, long ear ornaments composed of clusters of tassels and proportionately massive neck chains supporting tiers of sculptural pendants. In vestiary sumptuosity, the Lady of Elche could have held her own at the court of any pharaoh. The Phoenicians were technically accomplished workers in gold; it is believed that they invented the texturing known as granulation. Beyond the Mediterranean world, goldsmiths in Troy and other wealthy metropolitan centers of what is now Anatolia, or Asiatic Turkey, fashioned crude but powerfully evocative jewels, such as a necklace of great golden spangles found in the famous pre-Hittite royal tombs at Alaça Hüyük (plate 7).

Homer sang of the archaic pre-Hellenic city of Mycenae as "rich in gold," and modern archaeological finds have confirmed the characterization. Mycenae did indeed abound in gold, and her artificers excelled in the working of the precious metal. They favored *repoussé* work, done in spiral or chevron patterns and an early version of the angular Greek fret (plate 8); and like other jewelers of the time, they also depicted in bas-relief such creatures of land and sea as the butterfly, the starfish and the cuttlefish. It is notable that even in Mycenae the rendering of these motifs (and an occasional rendering of the human figure, although it was still shown in profile) reveals an impulse toward three-dimensional plasticity that is clearly premonitory of Greek art.

Fortunately, it was these aesthetic impulses of the Mycenaeans, rather than their other, ruder characteristics, that were absorbed by their Hellenistic successors. Centuries later, when Sophocles (496?–406 B.C.) echoed the Homeric apostrophe, he would temper it with a reference to Mycenae's royal palace "drenched with blood." In the gentler age of Sophocles, Phidias and Pericles, barbarisms of the past were execrated as fervently as art and literature were praised. The mild and noble genius of Greece is reflected in her jewels as in her laws, her writing, her architecture and her sculpture. More exactly, the jewelry of ancient Greece *is* architecture and sculpture—carried out on a miniature scale and in virgin gold rather than marble.

This phenomenon is demonstrated most convincingly perhaps in the pendent earring, the form on which the fame of Greek jewelry ultimately rests (plates 9 and 10). But the sculptural element is hardly lacking in any form; it is particularly evident, for instance, in the

7.
This surprisingly modern-looking gold necklace was created not by an avant-garde jeweler but by an ingenious pre-Hittite craftsman of the third millennium B.C. Anatolian, Alaça Hüyük, Turkey, c. 2400–2300 B.C. Archaeological Museum, Ankara

8.
The vermiculate repoussé pattern on this gold disk evolved into the familiar Greek fret encountered so often in jewelry decoration throughout later centuries. Mycenaean, Syria, c. 1500 B.C. Seattle Art Museum, gift of Mr. and Mrs. William Garrard Reed

9

10

11

9.
Right side view of an unusually large and complex gold earring pendant, a splendid example of sculptural mastery applied to jewelry decoration. The composition represents Nike (or Victory) driving a chariot; the motif above the figure's head is a variation of the classical honeysuckle palmette. Greek, fourth century B.C. Museum of Fine Arts, Boston, H. L. Pierce Fund

10.
The graceful Nike depending from the classical rosette of this single earring may have originally held drapery in one hand and a wreath in the other. Figure, solid cast gold; details, sheet gold and filigree. Greek, late fourth century B.C. Virginia Museum of Fine Arts, Richmond, Williams Fund

11.
A gold medallion disk centering a bust of Athena. The limited number of cabochon garnets in the outer ring (one still remains) and the plain arcs of garnets held by gold loops in the ring around the bust are representative of the restrained use of semiprecious inlays and cabochon gems in Greek jewelry. Possibly Thessalian, late third–early second century B.C. The Art Museum, Princeton University, Princeton, N.J.

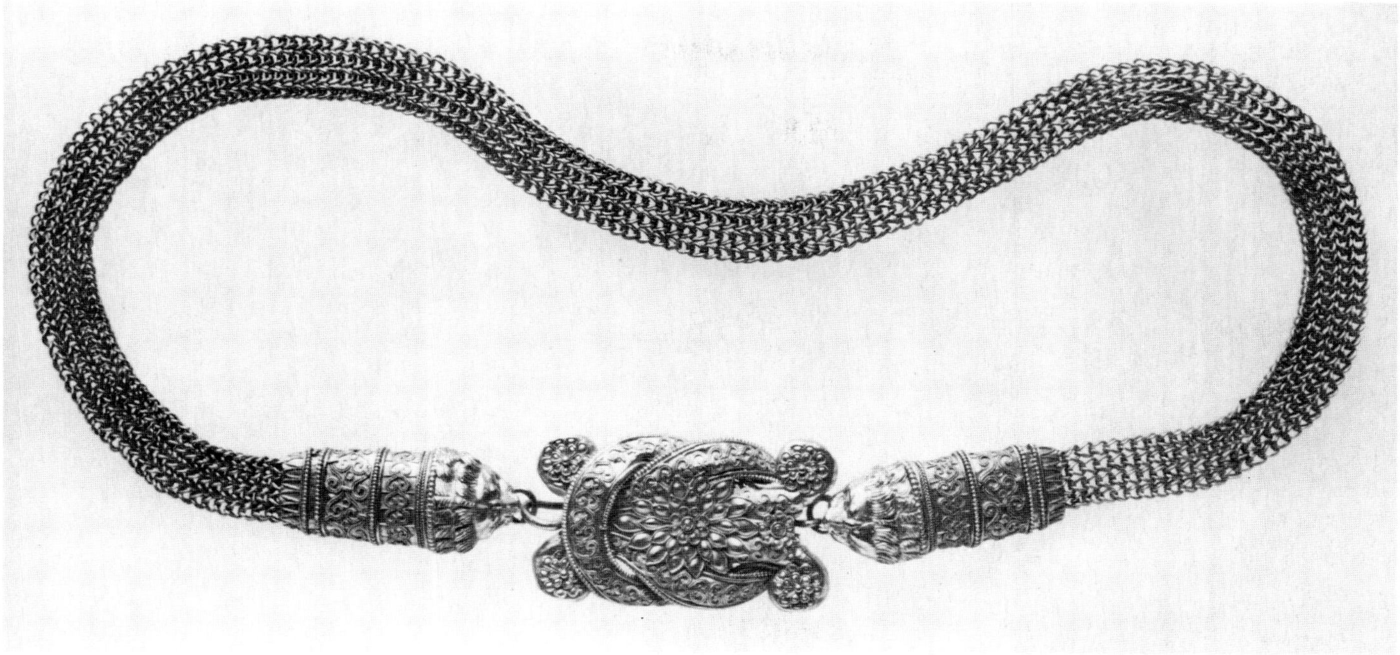

12

13

12.
A gold thigh band with a centerpiece in the shape of a Hercules knot that appears to be a buckle but serves only to hide the closure. This decorative feature and the terminals of the band are covered with filigree, except for the boldly sculptural lion heads. Greek, late fourth century B.C. Staatliche Antikensammlungen, Munich

13.
A classical Greek gold necklace, with bud and amphora pendants held by rosettes. A type of necklace that has been defined as "simplicity itself—a strap with a fringe," it nevertheless displays an astonishing complexity of detail. Greek, probably Asia Minor, fourth–third century B.C. Metropolitan Museum of Art, New York, 1899

14.
One of a pair of gold hoop earrings with goat-head finials. The naturalistic representation of the animal is such that it might almost be termed a portrait. Italo-Greek, sixth century B.C. Los Angeles County Museum of Art, gift of Mr. and Mrs. Alan C. Balch

Colorplate 5.
Top left: A gold comb with figures that have a strong three-dimensional effect despite being worked in bas-relief. Conception and execution are Greek, but the clothing and accouterments are unmistakably Scythian, as is the mood of savage drama. Ukraine, early fourth century B.C. State Hermitage Museum, Leningrad
Top right: A Scythian medallion pendant of gold and enamel, inspired by the *Athena Parthenos* of Phidias. Traces of delicate blue enameling still persist in the rosettes and amphorae that hang from the disk. Scythian, Crimea, fourth century B.C. State Hermitage Museum, Leningrad
Bottom: A gold pectoral with cords of plaited gold and pinecone tassels that bespeak Greek influence. The repoussé work and the fibulae (primitive forerunners of safety pins) are barbarian characteristics. Thracian, late sixth century B.C. Archaeological Museum, Plovdiv, Bulgaria

medallion disk in high relief shown in plate 11, one of a group of similar extant disks. Generally believed to have been utensil covers, these small circular plaques are now thought by some scholars to have been "body jewelry"—either breast coverings held in place by crossed straps or the tops of chignon coifs, the small rings on their peripheries serving to hold "nettings" or "hairnets" of gold chains.

This furnishes an interesting example of present-day uncertainty about the function of particular items of antique jewelry. What is now called a thigh band (plate 12) was long mistaken for a necklace of sorts, even though the typical necklace form consists of a band, or chain, fringed with at least one tier of small pendants (plate 13) in such shapes as amphorae, acorns, shells, human masks or animal heads. Some of these motifs had been derived by Greece from Asia (for instance, the amphora), as had hoop earrings with animal heads (plate 14) and penannular bracelets (bracelets in the form of an incomplete circle), also with animal heads as finials.

One of the handsomest and most original of all Greek jewelry designs is the snake bracelet. This could be utterly simple, forming a single loop around the limb, but the design could also be astonishingly intricate. In one remarkable example (plate 15), a pair of serpents entwine their bodies in a complex coil that forms the symbolic Hercules knot.

Mention was made earlier of the custom of adorning the dead with jewels created specifically for the purpose. Unlike the magnificent treasures accompanying Tutankhamun into the netherworld, however, most funerary jewelry was flimsily and inexpensively made since it would not need to withstand actual wear. This custom was widespread in the Mediterranean region, including Greece. It is precisely because of their frailty that Hellenistic mortuary ornaments are devoid of even a hint of morbidity. The naturalistic wreaths of foliage made of gold foil that have survived are surpassingly lovely—fitting jewelry indeed for travelers to the Elysian Fields (plate 16).

As early as the seventh century B.C., Greek jewelers disseminated Hellenic culture by traveling afar and, apparently in an effort to satisfy foreign patrons, tackled bold new themes, achieving intriguing results. Thus a pectoral found in ancient Thrace (which corresponds roughly to modern European Turkey, northeastern Greece and parts of Yugoslavia and Bulgaria) consists of a plate of hammered gold and two sturdy *fibulae*—a typical barbarian conception, as we shall see in the next chapter—with an unexpectedly graceful detail: gold chains ending in pinecone tassels, a characteristically Greek touch (colorplate 5).

In time, in the more remote and even wilder land of the Scythians to the north of Thrace, some forgotten Greek genius succeeded in effecting an almost perfect fusion of Hellenistic skill and barbarian

COLORPLATE 5

inspiration. It might seem that an example of Greek lyricism as perfect as the Athena pendant shown at top right in colorplate 5 could not be surpassed. But conventional visions of Olympus did not satisfy the ancient dwellers of the vast steppes where the Zaporozhe Cossacks would later roam. Instead, these northerners evidently wished to have records of their daily activities portrayed in terms of Greek art and skill, but with complete fidelity to their own culture. The poetry and realism thus blended in gold and enamel, or in solid gold,

15.
In this superb gold and garnet bracelet, the loveliest and most intricate version of the Greek snake bracelet known today, twin serpents coiling in opposite directions entwine their tails in a Hercules knot. Small jewels, now missing, may have sparkled in the eye sockets. Greek, fourth–third century B.C. Schmuckmuseum, Pforzheim, West Germany

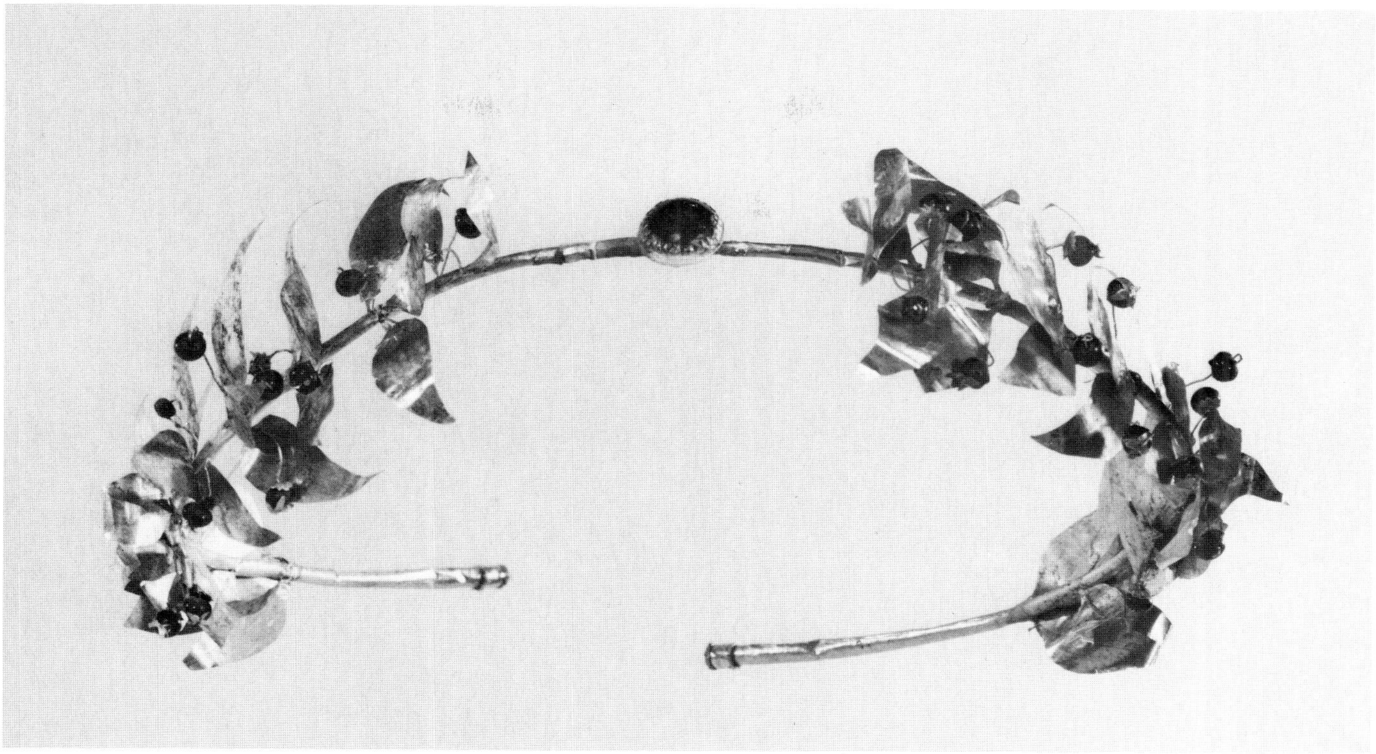

16.
A funerary myrtle wreath of gold and garnet. Because its construction is sturdier than was usual for wreaths of this nature, this piece may have been designed for actual wear rather than as a mortuary token. Greek, Amphipolis, Macedonia, third century B.C. Virginia Museum of Fine Arts, Richmond, Williams Fund

resulted in pieces that may well be ranked among the world's most admirable jewels (colorplate 5, comb, and colorplate 6).

In the seventh century B.C., at the time when the Hellenes were starting their rise to timeless fame, there lived in Italy, in what is now Tuscany and part of Umbria, an already ancient people, the mysterious Etruscans. Where they came from originally we do not know, but they have left ample proof of a culture of extraordinary character and vitality. No Etruscan relics are more intriguing than their rich and complex jewelry, notably of gold. Etruria had no gold, though she was rich in other minerals; gold was brought there, together with the rudiments of the knowledge to work it, by Greek traders.

Notwithstanding their late start, the Etruscans proved such apt pupils that they soon surpassed their teachers. They became renowned especially for granulation—the technique involving the use of minute globules of gold that was also known to the Phoenicians and the Greeks but was highly refined by the Etruscans. Early Etruscan jewelry—for instance, a fine fibula decorated with a frieze of wild animals (plate 17)—combines robustness of form with extreme delicacy of ornamentation, a combination that might well be regarded as basic to all good jewelry design. In this piece and in a pendant (plate 18) of the bearded head of the river god Achelous, the granulation, if

Colorplate 6.
Modeled by an unknown Greek master, this massive collar of virgin gold is 1 foot (30.5 cm.) in diameter and weighs approximately 2¼ pounds (1.02 kg.). Its forty-eight human and animal figures present the dual aspects of Scythian life and character: in the upper tier, the pastoral; in the lower, the fierce and wildly imaginative. South Russia, fourth century B.C. Kiev Historical Museum

not microscopic, as admirers are often wont to say, is certainly of particular fineness. The Etruscans also favored another globular element in their jewelry that seems at times inordinately large: the *bulla*—from a Latin word meaning "bubble," though this device was not always spherical (plate 19). Decoration with bullae, granulation or filigree serves one purpose—the variegation of textures. And an awareness of texture is of course related to an awareness of color. The Greek jewelers, more intellectual than their Etruscan counterparts, were primarily devoted to gold and to sculptural values, and introduced but very subtle color touches: a bit of restrained enameling here, a cabochon gem (usually garnet) there. The Etruscans, more emotional, and in a sense more primitive, were not averse to combining gold with sizable amounts of such semiprecious substances as amber or agate, or imitations of these in glass (plate 20), as well as with animal teeth and claws. Nor did Etruscan designers shun a certain massiveness of form, which does lend their work its special character but which Greek designers might well have found inharmonious. This massiveness was probably an expression of Etruscan energy and love of life, a national trait condemned by the Romans of the early republican era, who branded the Etruscans to the north as dissolute and disorganized—much too fond of jewelry, for example—and who ultimately brought about their downfall. Yet if Etruria was obliterated as a nation by Rome, and her culture erased, her people were inevitably incorporated in the body politic of Rome and of Italy as a whole, endowing all Italy with their virtues as well as their shortcomings.

We can only conjecture how much of the Etruscan skill and spirit later showed itself in Roman jewelry. We know that Roman jewelry was of Greek inspiration, since the Romans acknowledged, nay venerated, the intellectual and artistic superiority of Hellas. But

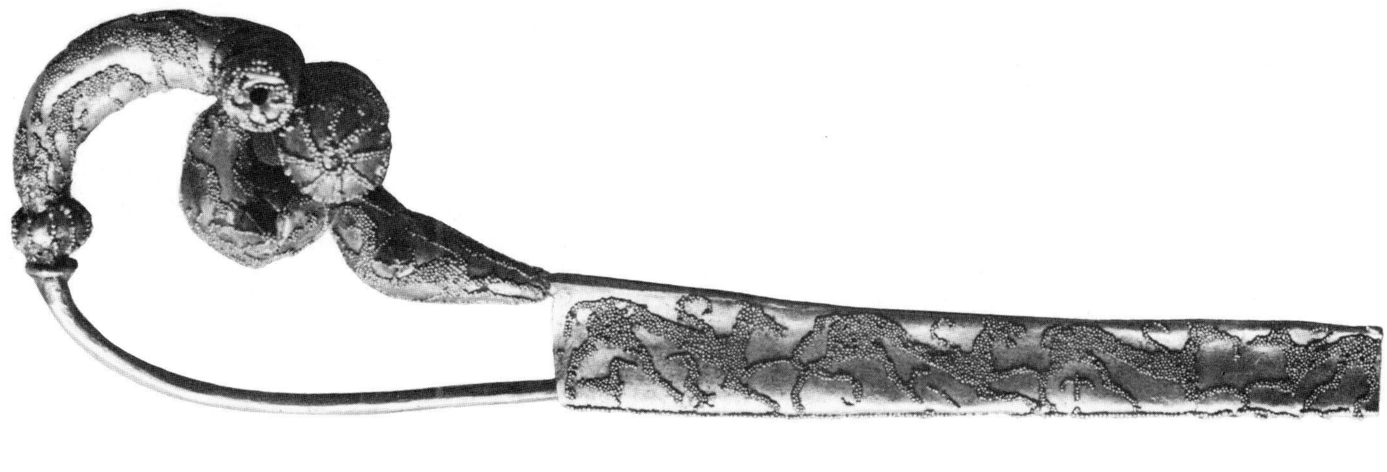

17.
A seventh-century B.C. gold fibula from the ancient Etruscan city of Rusellae. The shadowy frieze of animals is done in the granulation technique for which Etruscan jewelers were famous. Metropolitan Museum of Art, New York, 1895

18

20

19

18.
Probably the most famous example of Etruscan jewelry, this gold pendant depicting the head of the river god Achelous is notable for both vigor of conception and refinement of execution. Fifth century B.C. Louvre, Paris

19.
One of a pair of gold earrings employing the characteristic Etruscan bulla in a pyramidal cluster. Etruscan, fourth–third century B.C. Metropolitan Museum of Art, New York, funds from various donors, 1918

20.
A necklace of gold-mounted glass beads and gold pendants set with glass imitating banded agate and other semiprecious stones. This impressive piece is part of a set of jewelry unearthed at Vulci, Italy, about 1832. Etruscan, sixth–fifth century B.C. Metropolitan Museum of Art, New York, Harris Brisbane Dick Fund, 1940

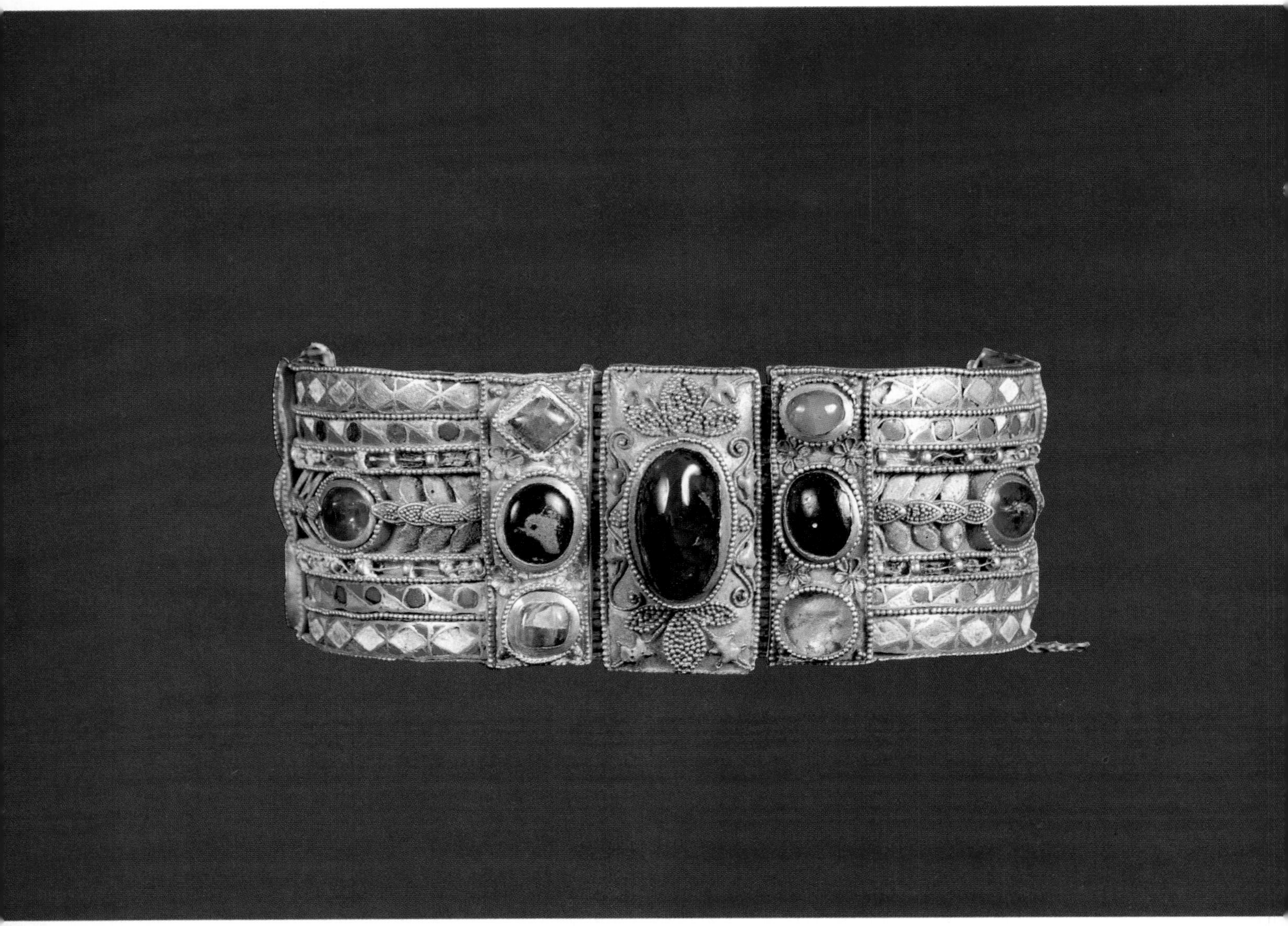

Colorplate 7.
Exemplifying the eclectic nature of Roman jewelry is this hinged gold armband found at the site of ancient Olbia on the Black Sea. The abundance of cabochon gems is of Oriental character; the tiered geometric inlays are barbarian; and the crude gold beading relates to Greece. Enamel, garnets, amethysts, other stones. Roman, first century A.D. Walters Art Gallery, Baltimore

Colorplate 8.
A Byzantine hinged bracelet of gold with pearls and soft-hued sapphires. Note the basic similarity of its design to that of the bracelet in plate 21. Byzantine, Constantinople (Istanbul), first half of the seventh century A.D. Metropolitan Museum of Art, New York, gift of J. Pierpont Morgan, 1917

21.
One of a pair of matching gold bracelets found in Cyprus, executed in the ancient Roman goldsmithing technique of *opus interrasile*, a delicate yet sturdy tracery. The large circular medallion acts as a clasp. Byzantine, probably Syrian, sixth century A.D. Metropolitan Museum of Art, New York, gift of J. Pierpont Morgan, 1917

22.
A Roman necklace of gold and glass, Hellenic in inspiration. Hercules knots bearing classical rosettes alternate with trios of glass beads; a lobed ornament hangs at the center. Roman, c. third century B.C. Smithsonian Institution, National Collection of Fine Arts, gift of John Gellatly

Roman jewelry nevertheless has a character of its own. Though relatively little of this work has survived, we know from historical records that it was sumptuous in the extreme, lavish in the use of gems. In republican times there had been an almost puritanical restraint, but under the empire, with the world's wealth pouring into the capital city, luxury knew no bounds. The emperor Nero (A.D. 37–68) is said to have owned a monocle with a lens made of emerald. Such extravagances could have occurred only at the very apex of the social pyramid; but historians tell of ordinary mortals seeking to rival the ruling families, among them a Roman matron who attended a simple betrothal ceremony bedecked from head to toe with pearls and emeralds. Earrings with pendants composed of multiple pear-shaped pearls were called *crotalia*, a term evidently derived from *crotala*, meaning rattles or castanets, which indicates that pleasure was taken in the sound as well as the look of pendent pearls. Since men were still somewhat limited by a Roman tradition that frowned upon jewels for males, signet rings were in great favor, and some were huge.

The very ornateness of Roman jewelry helped to spell its doom. In subsequent centuries the precious stones were removed so that they could be sold, and the heavy gold settings were melted down. We can only surmise from the few, relatively modest items to escape such destruction that Roman jewelry was eclectic in style, assimilating more or less successfully many contrasting elements borrowed from subject peoples—as, for example, in the sumptuously decorated armband shown in colorplate 7. At least one Roman contribution to the art of jewelry, however, deserves special attention. This was a technique known as *opus interrasile*, in which sheets of solid gold were pierced in lacelike patterns. In delicacy, the new Roman technique may not have been on a par with filigree, but in other ways it was superior: more variety of design was possible, and the open tracery was much sturdier. *Opus interrasile* was used to excellent advantage in the mounting of gold coins and cameos. The effects achieved were perhaps too rich, if not gross, in terms of Greek taste, but they called for considerable skill. An example of Byzantine use of this technique is illustrated in the sixth-century bracelet seen in plate 21.

One is tempted to conclude that at a certain stage Roman jewelry ceased to be primarily art and became decoration instead—decoration on as ostentatious a scale as could be afforded. For instance, contemporary commentators describing the jewels of the wife of the emperor Caligula (A.D. 12–41) did not mention their exquisite workmanship and beautiful design but emphasized the fact that the giant pearls and gems she wore in such profusion were worth a fortune.

For those who could not afford the genuine article, glass paste of remarkable quality was produced in Rome and also across the Mediterranean in Alexandria. In the form of beads, this paste was openly incorporated in precious jewelry (plate 22), and it was used also to simulate

Colorplate 9.
A double-sided clasp of gold with cloisonné enamel, its severe and lovely Madonna reflecting the religious themes that pervaded Byzantine life and art. The chastened elegance and striking monumentality of this miniature object are particularly noteworthy. Byzantine, Constantinople (Istanbul), tenth century A.D. Dumbarton Oaks Collection, Washington, D.C.

23.
Detail from a mosaic wall decoration in the Basilica of San Vitale in Ravenna, portraying the empress Theodora (center) in her imperial splendor. She wears an elaborate diadem and a capelike collar, both studded with huge gems and overflowing with streams of pearls. Byzantine, sixth century A.D.

Colorplate 9

24.
One of a pair of large drop earrings with seven stones and pearls set in gold and three amethyst pendants on gold wires, each with a green glass bead above it; found in Spain. Byzantine or Visigothic, sixth century A.D. Walters Art Gallery, Baltimore

precious stones. Indeed, in an age when the faceting of gems was as yet unknown, glass often surpassed stones in beauty and brilliance.

In A.D. 313, the emperor Constantine (280?–337) officially sanctioned the Christian religion in Rome. One might expect that this move would have affected the prevailing attitude toward extravagances of various sorts, including jewelry, but this was not the case, despite the clearly voiced pronouncements of Christian leaders. In fact, when Constantine established the new capital of the empire at Byzantium in 330, the closer contact with Persia and India brought about an even greater interest in jewelry that was elaborate in character and studded with precious stones.

We can be sure that the few Byzantine jewels that have survived hardly begin to give us an idea of the lavish jewelry of the Empire of the East. Very likely they are not even the tip of the proverbial iceberg but a mere sliver from a minor floe, the rest having long ago melted away. Still, some notion can be formed from such pictorial records as the famous Ravenna mosaics showing Justinian the Great (483–565) and his empress, Theodora. The emperor is portrayed wearing a diadem and a large jeweled brooch or clasp that holds the folds of his mantle at the shoulder—both objects exceedingly rich, though modest in comparison with those bedecking his consort. Theodora not only has on the same two-tiered crown as her spouse but on top of it she wears a sort of jeweled miter and below it a coif encrusted with large pearls, from which cascade streams of pearls again, with huge ovoid pendants (plate 23). Her collar is not merely broad but actually capelike, and its network of pearls is interspersed with massive plaques, apparently set with gems. What often passes unnoticed is that she also wears a necklace of large emeralds close around her throat; this was perhaps a personal jewel, as opposed to her sumptuous imperial regalia.

As reproduced in the mosaics, the regalia of the emperor and empress appears to be as heavy and somber as it is magnificent. In

reality, it may have been much softer and more graceful. We can assume so because a few examples of royal adornment in the imperial Byzantine style have survived from a later period. These include eleven votive crowns of pure gold, presented to a Spanish shrine by various seventh-century Visigothic kings of Spain, which were discovered in 1858 near Toledo. Perhaps the loveliest is the crown of Recceswinth (reigned 653–72), for its combination of buttercup yellow gold, violet-toned sapphires and milk-white pearls produces what has been described as "an exceedingly harmonious effect of color." Much the same terms might be used to describe a Byzantine bracelet of the early seventh century, similarly enriched with an apparently favorite scheme of sapphires, pearls and gold (colorplate 8, page 35).

Byzantine costume, influenced by both Oriental modes and Christian mores, included long sleeves, yet bracelets were still worn. Like the one in colorplate 8, they were generally large bands and usually had hinged halves. Roman cutout work was often used (plate 21). Earrings also continued to be worn, one popular type being of hoop-and-crescent design—actually a circular medallion with an indentation at the top to accommodate the earlobe. Drop earrings with tiers of gems appear to have been both rich and elegant (plate 24). Girdles to gather the heavy folds of long gowns often consisted of circular medallions or plaques of other shapes joined by chain links (plate 25).

The chief glory of Byzantine jewelry, however, is the exquisite cloisonné enameling for which the craftsmen of Byzantium are justly famous (colorplate 9) and which, like all Byzantine artistic work, faithfully reflects the increasingly important role of color. Here we must keep in mind the influence of the new Christian iconography, which ruled out as immodest the plastic nudity of classical antiquity. Even when draped, the sensuously rounded forms of Greek art were condemned, to be replaced by severely linear interpretations that symbolized rather than actually represented the human figure. Only color could have afforded relief to such visual austerity.

25.
Part of a gold girdle from Cyprus, consisting of linked circular medallions with imperial themes. On the larger disks, the emperor appears in his chariot; on the smaller, he sits alone or with his consort. Byzantine, probably Syrian, sixth century A.D. Metropolitan Museum of Art, New York, gift of J. Pierpont Morgan, 1917

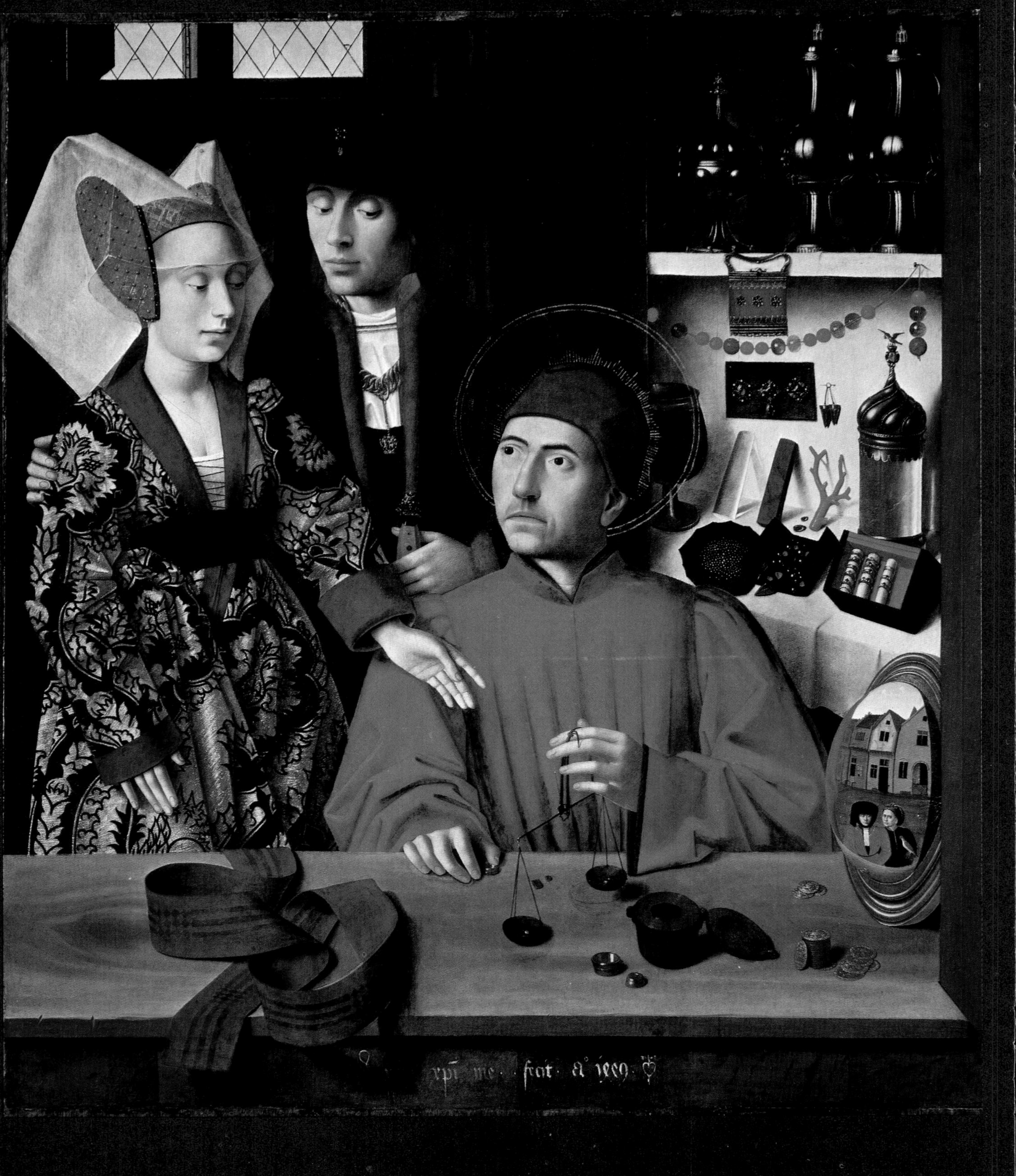

3 The Middle Ages

Imperial Rome may be said to have collapsed about A.D. 400, and we regard the next five centuries as the Age of Tribal Migrations, or of Barbarian Invasions. These terms are particularly suitable to describe the jewelry of the period, for these objects are indeed products of the human tides that, for generation after generation, swept back and forth across the territory that would in time be parceled out into the nations of Europe.

Attila the Hun (A.D. 406?–453), leader of the fiercest of the invading tribes, called himself the Scourge of God, and according to the devastation said to have been left in his wake, he was just that. Attila's Huns and other invaders from the north and east grew rich on their spoils, and much of the plundered wealth was in the form of, or converted into, jewels, of which the invaders were at least as fond as were the peoples they overran. They, too, buried their dead in graves furnished with objects that had been precious or useful to the departed, and these of course included jewels in proportion to the dead person's rank in life. Such funerary hoards were likely to include not only jewels made by the invaders but others obtained by pillage or by trade, so that exact ethnic identification is often impossible—as is the dating of such hoards, since even the inclusion of coins of known dates is not necessarily a reliable index.

The invaders of Teutonic stock were migrants, not nomads, and unwilling migrants at that, who had been driven to move southward and westward because of the pressure on their borders of even more aggressive peoples from the east. Their aim was to find and settle in safe new homelands, which is what the Franks and Burgundii did in Gaul, the Ostrogoths and Lombards in Italy, the Visigoths in Spain. In time, they renounced their pagan divinities and became at least nominal Christians. This did not make for peace, as internecine wars continued to rage; but in one respect at least the newcomers helped

Colorplate 10.
Saint Eligius, or Éloi (A.D. 588?–659), at once a goldsmith and a royal minister, who became the patron saint of goldsmiths and jewelers, is portrayed in a shop crowded with the wares and tools of the craft. The setting, however, is of the period of the artist, Petrus Christus (1420?–1473). *The Legend of Saint Godebertha and Saint Eligius*, Flemish, signed and dated 1449. Metropolitan Museum of Art, New York, Robert Lehman Collection, 1975

to establish, or reestablish, elements of a settled culture, by bringing with them into Europe half-forgotten traditions of a decorative art harking back to the dawn of human history in Asia. It is especially evident in the robust, stylized treatment of animal forms common to many primitive peoples. The bird shape in particular (colorplate 11 and plate 26) was as much a totemic symbol for the Germanic tribes as the elk had been for the Scythians.

As in all primitive cultures, the artifacts made by the migrants—and primarily their jewels, on which of course they lavished great care—are marked by a combination of simple, basic forms and intricate surface decorations favoring repeated geometric patterns and curvilinear designs: coils, spirals, vermiculations and the like (plates 27, 28 and 29). Such characteristics have endured to the present day, with only slight regional variations, in the peasant, or folk, jewelry of Europe.

What endows many of the jewels of the invaders with a tang of savage splendor is the technique of decoration employed. This was not liquid enameling by means of vitreous flux, as had been used in the Byzantine enamels (see colorplate 9, page 39), but solid inlay—slabs of some variety of garnet, perhaps almandine, or even glass, cut exactly to the shape of predesigned partitions (plate 26). This technique is similar to the Egyptian form of inlaying (see the earrings and pectorals in colorplate 3, page 17). Another characteristic of the jewelry of the Age of Tribal Migrations and Barbarian Invasions is its practical nature, its utility. If the broad collar was the distinctive jewel of Egypt, the earring that of Greece and the finger ring that of Rome, the fibula—that ancient ancestor of the safety pin, which we encountered earlier in Thrace and Etruria—was that of barbarian Europe. Even the archaic Etruscan bow type was still in use among the Huns (plate 30), but the arbalest type, as in a magnificent Ostrogothic example (colorplate 12), was more usual. The radiated-head fibula (plate 27) is a variation of the T-shaped type, while the circular fibula (plate 28) clearly comes closest to our modern brooch.

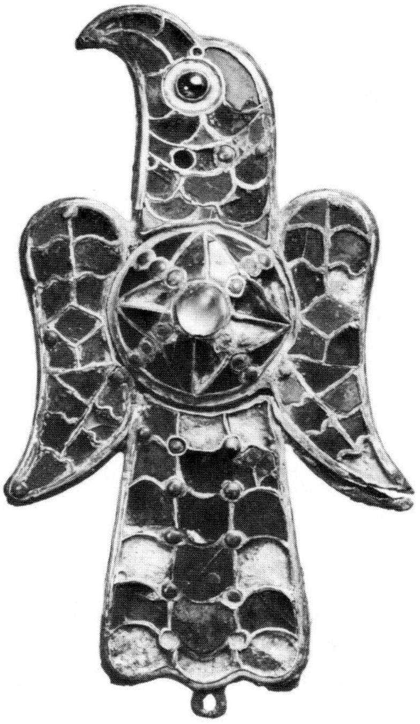

26.
One of a pair of gilt-bronze fibulae of eagle shape, with characteristic inlay of various materials: garnets, glass paste and stones. Visigothic, Spain, second half of the sixth century A.D. Walters Art Gallery, Baltimore

Next in importance to the fibula must rank the belt buckle (plate 29), which was worn by both sexes. Other than that, we have little information about the feminine adornments of the time, although utilitarian or purely decorative jewelry was surely not reserved for male warriors alone. Chroniclers of Frankish rule in western Europe, for instance, do not fail to mention that the beautiful, fierce queens Fredegunde (d. A.D. 597) and Brunhilda (d. A.D. 613) were always accompanied by their jewel caskets, though the jewels themselves are not described. We know that Brunhilda's sister, the Visigothic princess Galswintha (d. A.D. 567), was spared her life for a brief while because her husband, Chilperic I (d. A.D. 584), was impressed by the rich dowry in jewels she had brought from her native Iberia; though

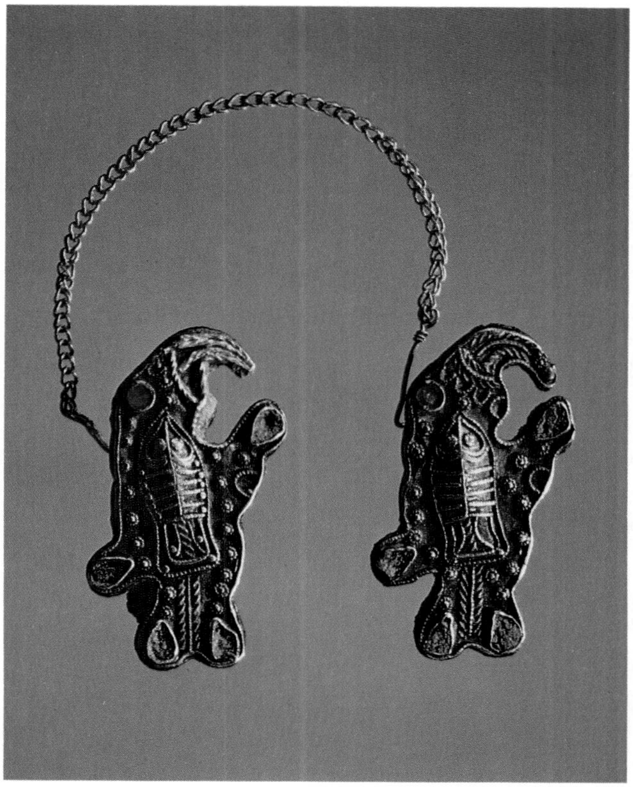

COLORPLATE 11

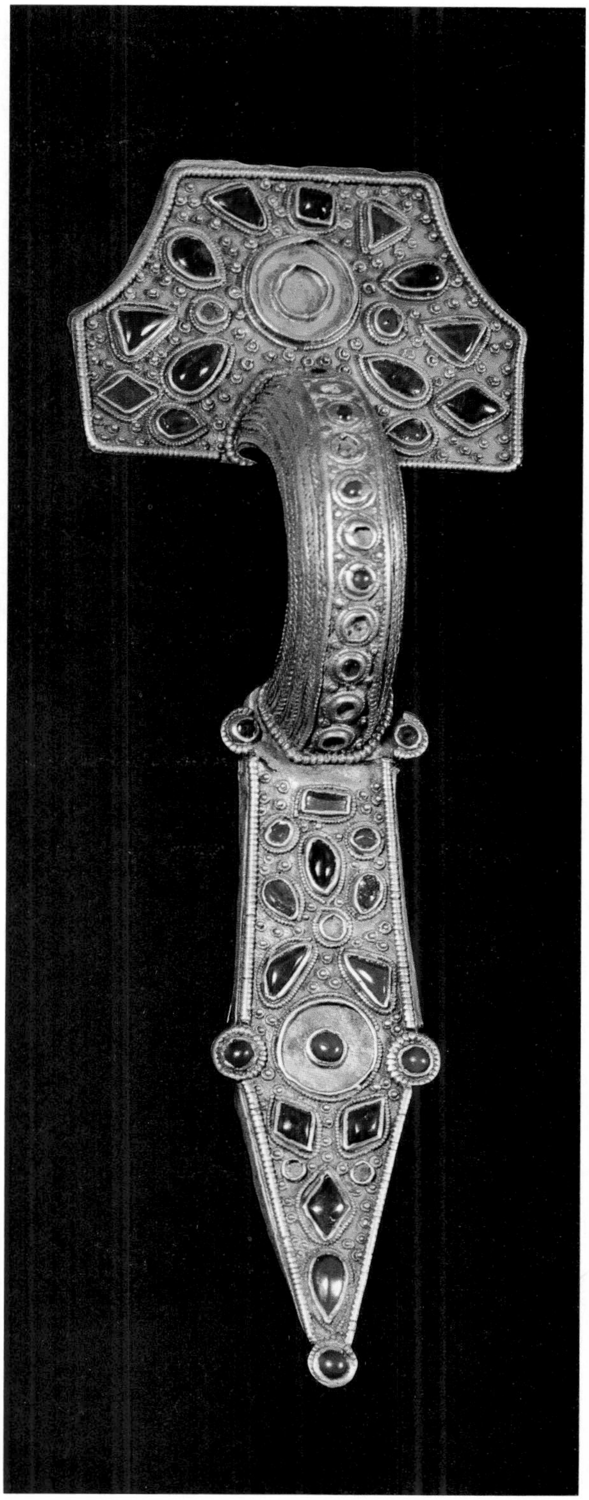

COLORPLATE 12

Colorplate 11.
A matching pair of gold-plated bronze fibulae in the form of stylized birds, decorated with red and blue-gray inlays. Probably totemic symbols of good luck, the pieces exhibit an unexpected and amusing surrealism: note the fish prey that the birds—probably a kind of kingfisher—have presumably just eaten. Frankish, Marchèlepot, France, first half of the seventh century A.D. Metropolitan Museum of Art, New York, gift of J. Pierpont Morgan, 1917

Colorplate 12.
An arbalest-type fibula with gold plates on a silver core encrusted with cabochon almandines. The Ostrogothic migrations have left few jeweled remains of comparable magnificence and style. Ostrogothic, Transylvania, fourth century A.D. Metropolitan Museum of Art, New York, Fletcher Fund, 1947

27.
A radiated-head bow fibula, of silver gilt with typical barbarian ornamentation of knobs, spirals and frets. Alemannic, sixth century A.D. Metropolitan Museum of Art, New York, gift of Alastair Bradley Martin, 1948

28.
A circular fibula of gold with glass paste. Its form closely resembles the modern brooch. Merovingian, sixth–seventh century A.D. M. H. de Young Memorial Museum, San Francisco, gift of California Midwinter International Exposition, 1895

27

28

29.
A tinned-bronze belt buckle and plate, with incised strapwork designs against a hatched ground. The flat effect is similar to the look of niello work. The massive bosses of the plate are a familiar device. Frankish, seventh century A.D. Walters Art Gallery, Baltimore

again we do not know what the jewels were. The treasure Chilperic I took with him to his tomb, however, has been preserved, and is now on display at the Musée de Cluny in Paris. It includes three hundred golden bees that had bespangled the royal mantle. The practice of attaching jeweled ornaments to vestments is exceedingly ancient—we have already seen how small plaques of hammered gold ornamented the sashlike girdle of Tutankhamun's consort (plate 2, page 12).

The more recent the period, we might assume, the greater the amount of jewelry that would have survived. But like all rules, this one has its exceptions. It certainly does not hold true for jewelry from the Middle Ages. Beginning with the ninth century, there is a disappointing dearth of contemporary work. Yet this same century marked the height of the empire of the greatest of Frankish monarchs, Charlemagne (A.D. 742–814), when relative political and economic stability and close ties with Constantinople and the Orient might be supposed to have resulted in quantities of fine jewelry. One reason for the scarcity of surviving examples is to be found in an edict of Charlemagne's. Reformer as well as conqueror, and a devout Christian, Charlemagne condemned the pagan practice of burying the dead with

30.
A gold bow fibula in the form of a horse's head and mane. Hunnish, c. A.D. 400. Walters Art Gallery, Baltimore

their worldly possessions. As a practical administrator he deplored the economic loss to the living of burying such treasure, and as an autocrat he eventually forbade it outright. While this worked to the benefit of the emperor and his empire, it has also worked to our undoubted loss. Carolingian jewels that remained in private hands were exposed in the course of centuries to vicissitudes very few have weathered safely. As a result, what little remains is mostly ecclesiastical: crosses, *flabella* (fans used in ceremonies), tabernacles, reliquaries and the like (plate 31).

It is notable, however, that the emperor himself took with him into his tomb at Aix-la-Chapelle a historic jewel sometimes called the amulet of Charlemagne. The term is both inaccurate and disparaging, for the jewel is said to have been a reliquary pendant of particularly exalted sanctity. We know from a surviving illustration that it was a disk of gold, encrusted with gems surrounding a large oval cabochon sapphire. Beneath this sapphire lay what were reputed to be a fragment of the hair of the Virgin Mary and a sliver of the True Cross, given to the emperor by his good friend the caliph Harun al-Rashid. Some two or three centuries after the emperor's death, the pendant was removed from the imperial crypt and placed in the treasury of the cathedral at Aix-la-Chapelle. There it stayed until 1804, when it was turned over to the prospective Empress Josephine of France (1763–1814), to be worn at her coronation. It remained in the possession of the Bonaparte family until, shortly before her death in 1920, the widow of Napoleon III, the former Empress Eugénie, presented it to the Archbishop of Rheims to help compensate for the wartime damage done to the historic cathedral in 1914. Its present whereabouts are un-

31.
Delicate champlevé enameling embellishes this medieval flabellum. Gilt copper, silver and gold; set with cabochon gems. Under the central section is a niche for a sacred relic, now missing. German (Rhenish), c. 1200. Metropolitan Museum of Art, New York, Cloisters Collection, 1947

31

32

33

known, although as recently as 1952 Joan Evans, an authority on antique jewels, exerted every effort to locate it. One is tempted to surmise that somehow it has found its way back to the original owner.

Byzantine influence on the jewelry of early Western cultures was generally Oriental rather than Occidental, although elements of classical Roman grandeur were transmitted in a curious and somewhat questionable way. Roman cameos, carved with mythological or imperial subjects, were sometimes pawned off as emblems of Christian piety. For instance, a cameo of Jupiter with his eagle was said to be a likeness of Saint John the Evangelist, the Jovian bird becoming the symbol of the Beloved Disciple (plate 32). Another cameo, with a fine profile of Emperor Augustus (63 B.C.–A.D. 14), was mounted as a breast jewel on the reliquary bust of Saint Hilary (plate 33). By association, the beautiful head in this precious setting may very likely have passed among the unsophisticated as a semblance of the Lord himself. Again in the same mood, an inscription in Greek characters was incised at some later time along a profile portrait of Emperor Caracalla (A.D. 188–217) engraved on a fine aquamarine, identifying the image as being that of Saint Peter. The cropped curls and short bushy beard of the emperor's likeness corresponded in some measure to the traditional appearance of the Prince of the Apostles. Thus sanctified, the semblance of a notably wicked ruler graced the cover of an eleventh-century missal, which, like the Jupiter/Saint John cameo (plate 32), was presented to a venerated shrine by Charles V of France (Charles the Wise) near the end of the fourteenth century.

Some authorities believe that the crafts taught by early Christian missionaries in Ireland and Scotland were still practiced there even after Europe was engulfed by its barbarian invaders. It is to this presumed continuation of Byzantine tradition in such surviving enclaves of Romano-Celtic culture that the relative excellence of enamelwork in the British Isles is attributed, of which the most famous example is the Alfred jewel (plate 34), named for Alfred the Great (A.D. 849–899). Its delicate cloisonné enameling is protected by a plaque of rock crystal, and the mounting features beading and granulation. The inscription in Anglo-Saxon carved on the band has been translated as "Alfred ordered me to be made." There is difference of opinion, however, as to whether the jewel was actually made at home or purchased by Alfred on one of his trips to Rome, where high standards of craftsmanship, if not of art, were still maintained.

The characteristic insular ornament of the early Middle Ages is the Celtic penannular brooch. This type of fibula is very ancient: it has been found in prehistoric tombs, and may have been brought north-

32.
An antique Roman cameo of three-layer sardonyx, which was richly remounted by order of Charles the Wise for presentation to Chartres Cathedral in 1367. It is actually a portrait of Jupiter that became identified as Saint John the Evangelist. Gold setting with red and blue enameling. French, fourteenth century. Bibliothèque Nationale, Cabinet des Médailles, Paris

33.
The jewel of Saint Hilary, perhaps the most beautiful example of a medieval mounting of a classical carved gem. This brooch consists of a cameo profile of the emperor Augustus in sardonyx surrounded by a garland of rubies, sapphires and pearls set in silver gilt. French, late twelfth–early thirteenth century. Bibliothèque Nationale, Cabinet des Médailles, Paris

34.
The renowned Alfred jewel, with the figure of a man in cloisonné enamel under crystal. The enamelwork and the carved gold surround may be debased Byzantine work, but the granulated gold boar's head of the handle appears closer in style and workmanship to the jewels of the Tribal Migrations period. Seventh–ninth century A.D. Ashmolean Museum, Oxford

34

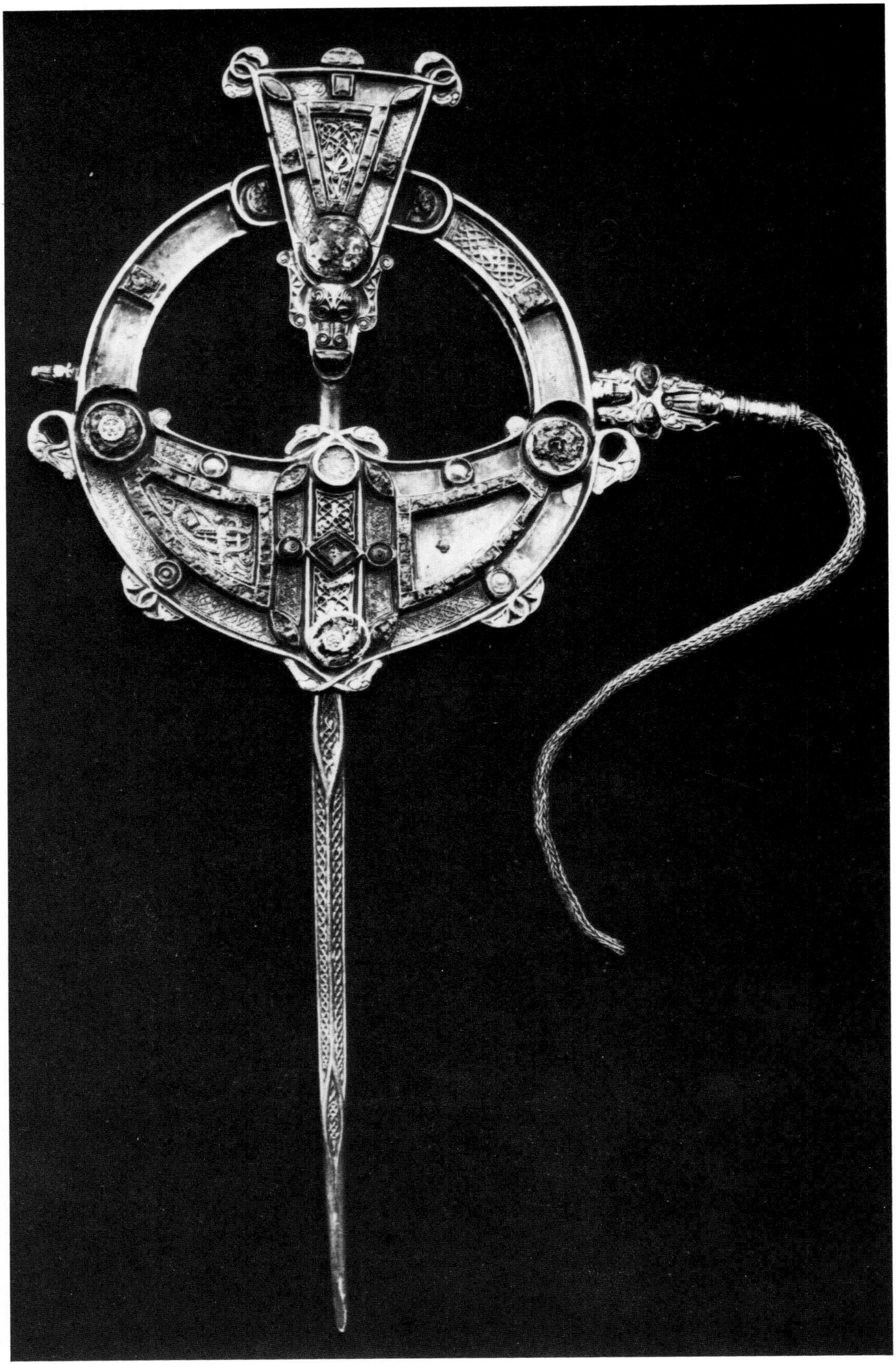

35

35.
The historic Tara brooch, famed for its unusual delicacy of execution and variety of decoration. It is of chased and engraved gilt bronze with inlaid gems, gold filigree and enamel. Each fragment of the complex cloisonné enameling was made separately, and the minute elements were then mounted like jewels. Celtic, Ireland, eighth century A.D. National Museum of Ireland, Dublin

ward by Celts migrating from what is now the Balkan area. A supreme example of the Celtic fibula is the Tara brooch, with decoration that could be described in modern parlance as multimedia, involving almost every jewelry technique known at the time (plate 35). While the Tara fibula is thought to date from the eighth century, penannular pins of this type were in use until the end of the thirteenth century; they were then replaced by pieces of a more or less similar shape with a hinged pin in back, known as *nouch* or *ouch*, and closely approximating our modern version of the brooch.

At about this period significant changes in vestiary customs were taking place. Garments in Mediterranean cultures were generally of one piece, to be draped or wrapped around the body, with the folds fastened by lacing or pinning. Hence Greeks and Romans who encountered invading barbarians were doubtless greatly surprised by their custom of wearing garments that encased the limbs separately—for instance, the trousers of the Scythians (see the comb in colorplate 5, page 27), or those of the Franks, which were laced at the ankle and sometimes all the way up to the knee. The usefulness of such garments in climates more rugged than those of Hellas and Italy was obvious; the tunic and the toga did not follow the spread of migrant cultures across Europe. Then with the gradual spread of Christianity came the concept of Christian modesty, along with that of the sinfulness of bare limbs and partial nudity. Once the practical and moral reasons for fitted garments had been realized, they were generally used, and by the mid-fourteenth century, buttons were the common fasteners.

For information on the jewelry of the period from the twelfth to

36.
Winged angels alternate with stylized fleurs-de-lis around a silver-gilt votive crown presented by Louis IX of France (Saint Louis) to the Dominicans of Liège sometime prior to 1270. French, thirteenth century. Louvre, Paris

37

37.
A great sapphire-studded fleur-de-lis gleams on the silver-gilt lozenge clasp that once held the royal mantle of Saint Louis. French, thirteenth century. Louvre, Paris

38.
The jeweled bridal crown, notable for its elegantly tall fleurons, worn by Princess Blanche, daughter of Henry IV of England, for her marriage to the Elector of Bavaria, Ludwig III, in 1402. French or English, c. 1370–80. Schatzkammer der Residenz, Munich, Wittelsbach Treasure

38

the fifteenth century, we must rely largely on portraits, statuary and so on, for very few actual jewels other than votive offerings and regalia have survived (plates 36, 37 and 38). Valuable documentation is furnished, for instance, in the depiction of a contemporary jeweler's workshop painted by the Flemish artist Petrus Christus (colorplate 10). By the fifteenth century, painters had become adept at portraying the clothing and ornaments worn by their subjects, and we therefore have a number of pictorial records of jewels (plates 39 and 40). It does not necessarily follow that these jewels ever existed; they may have been products of the artists' imaginations, introduced to express their creativity or to flatter the subjects. Yet because it was depicted with such painstaking accuracy, much of this painted jewelry appears convincingly real. In fact, the skill with which it is reproduced often cannot be fully appreciated without a magnifying glass. The royal crown laid at the feet of God the Son in the great van Eyck altarpiece

39

39.
In her portrait by the Master of Moulins, done when she was about three years old, Margaret of Austria, daughter of the emperor Maximilian I, wears a rich *enseigne* on her bonnet and a pendant at her breast. Suitable to her station, the jewels assume even greater importance because of the subject's small size. French School, c. 1483. Château de Versailles

40

40.
Maria Bonciani, the wife of the wealthy Italian banker Pièrantonio Baroncelli, wears two rings, a pendant brooch, a necklace and beads at the wrist in a portrait by the Master of the Baroncelli Portraits. Her poetic collaret of blooms may well have been one of the jeweled "garlands" that earned fame and a nickname for the great goldsmith-painter Domenico Ghirlandaio. Italian, 1476. Uffizi Gallery, Florence

VITA·SINE·MORTE·IN·CAPITE·
GAVDIV SÑ MERORE·A·DEXTRIS
IVVET SÑ·SENECTVTE·I·FRONT
SECVRITAS·SÑ·TIMORE·A·SINIS

41.
The crown at the feet of God the Son and the hem of his robe—a detail of the central panel of the famous van Eyck altarpiece, *The Mystic Lamb,* at Ghent. The elements of the crown and the gems and pearls encrusting the garment are rendered with painstaking, masterful realism. Flemish, early fifteenth century. Cathedral of Saint Bavon, Ghent

at Ghent (plate 41) is no mere working model for a goldsmith-jeweler. It appears to be an almost photographically faithful reproduction of an actual crown, and it can be compared with other royal crowns of the type, such as that worn by Princess Blanche, daughter of Henry IV of England, at her marriage to Elector Ludwig III of Bavaria in 1402 (see plate 38). Similarly, the great conical miter worn by the enthroned Savior in the altarpiece is a triple papal tiara of the sort actually used by pontiffs then. On the other hand, the crown of Hubert and Jan van Eyck's Madonna, in an adjoining panel, is frankly a poet's dream, combining pulsing stars with dew-fresh roses and lilies above a broad bandeau of pearls and gems. Yet the gem-laden circlets on the heads of the musician angels in still another panel might well have been the work of some master jeweler of the time (plate 42).

A portrait of a queen of Scotland (plate 43) by another great

42.
Detail of a panel of the van Eyck altarpiece at Ghent. The jeweled fillets worn by these angelic choristers might easily have served as models for actual contemporary pieces. Flemish, early fifteenth century. Cathedral of Saint Bavon, Ghent

43.
Margaret of Denmark, Queen of Scotland—a detail of the Trinity altarpiece by Hugo van der Goes at Holyrood Palace, Edinburgh. This portrait reflects accurately the royal elegance and vestiary sumptuosity of the later medieval era. Flemish, c. 1476. On loan to the National Gallery of Scotland, Edinburgh. Copyright reserved to Her Majesty the Queen

43

Flemish artist, Hugo van der Goes (1440?–1482), has raised intriguing questions about the actual existence of pictured jewels. The very same necklace that graces the slender neck of the queen is also depicted by van der Goes in his portrait of the daughter of a wealthy Italian banker settled in Bruges (Portinari altarpiece, Uffizi Gallery, Florence). We can hazard several guesses at this point, one of which is that the artist incorporated the necklace in both instances as a purely decorative element. It may have been of his own design—a *bijou imaginaire*.

The portrait of Queen Margaret is notable also for the splendid border of her gown, encrusted with huge table-cut gems alternating with pearls. However, not only were table-cut gems still a novelty then but stones of such size would doubtless have been sufficiently famous to be inventoried and very probably given a name of their own, even as the three matched rubies, also table-cut, belonging to Charles the Bold (1433–1477), last Duke of Burgundy, were known as the Three Brothers (or Brethren). It may well be that the ornaments on the gown were *verroterie* (made of glass). The term was not then used in the modern derogatory sense; it would correspond rather to our term costume jewelry. The use of glass gems, even on a royal gown, would be entirely in keeping with the new conception of jewelry as playing a supporting role to the costume as a whole. The purely decorative element now assumed paramount importance, independent of preciousness or of symbolic meaning. This idea is of course a significant development, one of the consequences being that from then on even genuine jewels would have a short lifespan, since they would be reset frequently in order to keep up with changes of fashion.

Apart from royal adornments, the chief items of jewelry during the early Middle Ages were brooches and rings (which are mainly what have survived), followed by utilitarian belt buckles and mantle clasps. The best of these, though items of daily wear, show how far behind Europe had already left not only its "dark ages" but also hieratic Byzantine rigidity. The flat Byzantine patterning has been replaced by a vigorous plasticity; indeed, an almost genial sense of life pulses in the masterly clasp attributed to the workshop of the French craftsman Nicolas of Verdun (colorplate 13).

Colorplate 13.
A gilt-bronze clasp assigned to the workshop of the great early medieval goldsmith Nicolas of Verdun. It is both an admirable efflorescence of Gothic sculpture and an outstanding example of metalworking. French (Mosan), c. 1210. Metropolitan Museum of Art, New York, Cloisters Collection, 1947

The term Gothic, when applied to jewelry as well as to architecture and other art forms of the age, seems to bear no relation whatever to the predatory Ostrogoths and Visigoths of history, and in fact its artistic manifestations did not begin to appear in the lands these invaders had overrun and looted until some centuries had elapsed. Gothic art ultimately touched little or nothing, however, that it did not endow with freshness and grace. As Greek jewelers were able to reflect in miniature the essence of the marvels of the Acropolis, so the jewelers of the Age of Cathedrals were able to echo that sublime "frozen music." Their work combines elements of the strong yet delicate

44.
A silver-gilt cope morse by the goldsmith Reinecke van Dressche. The elements of the tondo design—tiers of arches, columns and pendentives—help to explain why jewelry, particularly that of the Middle Ages, is sometimes called architecture in miniature. German, Minden, 1487. Kunstgewerbemuseum, Staatliche Museen Preussischer Kulturbesitz, West Berlin

architectural framework (plate 44), a wealth of graceful foliate forms (see plates 38 and 41), an apparently inexhaustible fantasy (colorplate 14, brooch) and of course a childlike confidence and faith (colorplate 14, cope morse).

Not until the fourteenth century do we encounter many of the intimate qualities most treasured in personal jewelry. Roaming the Near East during the Crusades, more than one rude European campaigner must have acquired for the first time some rudiments of taste and style. European art was enriched almost overnight by spoils seized in Constantinople when that great city was captured in 1204 during the Fourth Crusade, including examples of jewelry brought back from there. Moreover, significant technical advances were taking place in the field of enameling. Cloisonné, inherited from Byzantium, was superseded by *champlevé* ("lifted field"), so called because shallow troughs were created in a metal base and then filled with enamel flux; and by *basse-taille* ("low cutting"), in which translucent enamel was laid over engraved metal in such a way that the engraved designs showing through the vitreous film appeared as if modeled in the enamel (plates 45 and 46).

45.
A gold triptych pendant with side shutters open to reveal a thirteenth-century Italian onyx carving of the Nativity in the central panel. The inner surfaces of the shutters are peopled with scenes from the Scriptures done in *basse-taille* enamel on gold ground. French, late fifteenth century. Cleveland Museum of Art, purchase from the J. H. Wade Fund

46.
A circular pendant with a cameo portrait, possibly of Robert, Seigneur de Masmines, or Philip the Good, Duke of Burgundy, of chalcedony on gold repoussé ground with *basse-taille* enamel. This is a rare medieval example of a style of jewelry decoration that attained great vogue during the Renaissance (see plates 60 and 70). Franco-Burgundian, c. 1440. Schatzkammer der Residenz, Munich

45

46

These techniques eliminated much of the inherent flatness of enameled jewelry. Later still, enamel was applied not only to flat surfaces but to full forms as well. Thus *émail en ronde bosse* ("enamel in rounded relief") was developed—a technique sometimes called *émail en blanc* ("enamel in white"), a double appellation that is frequently confusing, as the process is not at all limited to the use of white pigment in the enameling. This second term came about because of the undoubted emphasis now given to white in the decorative scheme (colorplate 14).

By this means it had become possible to produce jewelry with enameled figures in high relief—casts of lilliputian, often actually three-dimensional actors, with hands and faces in opaque white enamel, but otherwise brightly polychromed. These faithfully represented the life of the times, whether in scenes reminiscent of the *Roman de la Rose* and the lays of the troubadours (colorplate 14, brooch), or in solemn and resplendent envisionings of the most sacred religious mysteries (colorplate 14, cope morse).

Colorplate 14.

Left: This admirable brooch of gold, enamel, ruby and pearls, depicting a beguiling pair of young lovers in a symbolic enclosed garden, belonged to Mary of Burgundy, wife of Maximilian I and mother of the child shown in plate 39. The fine workmanship exemplifies all the richness and complexity of *émail en ronde bosse*, with white opaque enamel used for the hands and faces of the small figures, and translucent blue enamel *en basse-taille* for their garments, over a ground delicately chased to indicate fabric texture. The pearls are mounted in the medieval manner, *à potence* (in transverse gallows clamps). Burgundian, mid-fifteenth century. Kunsthistorisches Museum, Vienna

Right: The central medallion of this large gold and enamel cope morse, with its grouping of the Trinity within a crown of thorns, shows dramatically beautiful use of opaque white enamel *en ronde bosse* for the two figures and the hovering dove. French, Paris, c. 1400. National Gallery of Art, Washington, D.C., Widener Collection

4 The Renaissance

The term Renaissance is one to conjure with, evoking images of courtly splendor and artistic excellence—factors conducive to the creation of truly great jewelry. It is not to be wondered at, therefore, that Renaissance jewels should be as highly regarded as any other artistic productions of the age. Yet the Renaissance did not develop merely in the pursuit of visual beauty. It arose through the rediscovery of the intellectual achievements of the ancient world and the rebirth of interest in them, and reflected a wish to emulate that world on philosophical and literary as well as aesthetic levels. As far as was possible, Renaissance artists drew their inspiration from the considerable body of painting, sculpture and architecture to be found in the lands once dominated by Greece and Rome. In the field of jewelry, however, they had no choice but to be totally individualistic and original, for they knew very little of the jewels of antiquity.

At this point we should recall once again the difference between a gem and a jewel. Some engraved gems of the classical period—cameos and intaglios, for instance—had been preserved and were greatly admired in Renaissance times. But most such pieces were unmounted gems, long ago deliberately divested of their settings, perhaps by looters. The scarcity of actual jewels is easily understood if one recollects that archaeology had not yet evolved as a science, that systematic excavations were a thing of the future and that such finds as were made were not only accidental but rare.

Nevertheless, Benvenuto Cellini (1500–1571), the illustrious goldsmith and jeweler of the Italian Renaissance, tells in his *Autobiography* how "certain hunters after curiosities"—evidently collectors and antiquarians in the modern sense—were able to acquire treasures unearthed by peasants working in Italian vineyards. Cellini lists "antique medals, agates, chrysoprases, carnelians, and cameos; also sometimes gems, as, for instance, emeralds, sapphires, diamonds and rubies," as

Colorplate 15.
A necklace with a pendant representing a sphinx, of gold, enamel, pearls and gems. The brilliance of the translucent red and green enameling makes it difficult to distinguish between the mounted gems and the vitreous incrustations. Probably Florentine, late sixteenth century. National Gallery of Art, Washington, D.C., Widener Collection

well as objects he himself purchased: a magnificent topaz and an emerald carved with the head of a dolphin. "Here," he says, "art equalled nature; [the topaz] was as large as a hazelnut, with the head of Minerva in a style of inconceivable beauty. I remember yet another precious stone different from these: it was a cameo engraved with Hercules binding Cerberus. Such was the beauty and the skill of its workmanship that our great Michelagnolo [Michelangelo] protested that he had never seen anything so wonderful." It should be noted that no mention is made of the settings or mountings of these gems; if they had existed, Cellini would almost certainly have commented on them.

An outline of the development of jewelry during the early and High Renaissance is in effect a roll call of Italian art. The reason is that the *bottega* of a goldsmith was often far more than the literal translation of the term ("workshop" or "shop") would indicate. Instead, it

47.
Renaissance goldsmiths at work in a palatial workshop, as depicted in a fresco in the studio of Francesco I de' Medici (1541–1587), Grand Duke of Tuscany. In the right foreground, Jacques Bilivelt, court jeweler, is at work on the crown of Tuscany; at left, on the table, are two more crowns and a papal miter. The fresco was painted by Alessandro Fei, called del Barbiere (1543–1592). Italian, c. 1570. Palazzo Vecchio, Florence

48.
The subject of *Portrait of a Gentleman*, by Bartolommeo Veneto, wears on his cap an *enseigne* enameled brightly with a figure of Saint Catherine leaning on her wheel and holding the palm of martyrdom. Detail. National Gallery of Art, Washington, D.C., Samuel H. Kress Collection

was a training school for would-be artists, as well as a "club" where they could meet with masters and patrons (plate 47).

The first avocation of Lorenzo Ghiberti (1378–1455), sculptor of the famous bronze doors of the baptistery of San Giovanni in Florence, was goldsmithing. On the other hand, painters who undertook the creation of jewels preferred the aspects of the craft—enameling, for example—that allowed them to put their painterly talents to best use. One such was the great artist Antonio Pollaiuolo (1429?–1498), who in his own day enjoyed equal fame as enamelist and as painter. Another outstanding practitioner of enameling was Ambrogio Foppa (c. 1446–1530?), called Caradossa, one of the finest medalists of the age, who specialized in *enseignes* (cap or hat badges). These same objects have become the trademark of Bartolommeo Veneto (at work 1502–46), a painter whose male sitters invariably sport richly enameled *enseignes*, whether actual jewels (and in that case conceivably Veneto's own handiwork) or mere figments of the artist's imagination (plate 48).

Filippo Brunelleschi (1377?–1446), the architect who in time raised the immense dome of the Cathedral of Florence, also started his career as a goldsmith, so it may be that the first structures he designed were not of mortar and marble but precious miniatures like the tabernacle shown in plate 49 and in colorplate 16. Similarly, it is possible that Luca della Robbia (1400?–1482), who began his education as a goldsmith, did not model his first flowery and leafy garlands out of clay but shaped them in gold for jewelry decorations such as the lacy surround of an Annunciation scene on a circular pendant (plate 55). Mention of garlands brings to mind the painter Domenico Ghirlandaio (1449–1494), who was known by this surname precisely because he was first a maker of "garlands" (*ghirlande*)—the jeweled coronals traditionally worn by affianced maidens and brides. In one of his portraits, Ghirlandaio has depicted two of the most beautiful jewels of the age, which may well have been his own creations (plate 51). His son Ridolfo (1483–1561) followed in his footsteps as both painter and goldsmith.

Colorplate 16.
A medallion, probably an *enseigne*, of gold and enamel, with a miniature tabernacle whose folding doors, or wings, are opened to reveal a depiction of Veronica's Veil. Inside the door panels are the Annunciation figures of the Angel Gabriel (left) and the Virgin; in the lunette, God the Father. Plate 49 shows the doors closed. Italian, c. 1480

Colorplate 17.
The reverse of a gold pendant, enameled with the combined arms of Poland and the Sforza family of Milan. The front has a carved sardonyx portrait of Bona Sforza, wife of Sigismund I of Poland. Made by Giovanni Jacopo Caraglio of Verona (c. 1500–1565); dated 1554

Colorplate 18.
An oval medallion pendant, with a pearl drop below the relief portrait of the Holy Roman Emperor Charles V in gold and enamel on a bloodstone (heliotrope) background with a trim of lapis lazuli and gold. Italian, mid-sixteenth century

The jewels in colorplates 16–18 and plate 49 are from the Metropolitan Museum of Art, New York, gifts of J. Pierpont Morgan, 1917

49

49.
Enseigne in colorplate 16, opposite, with tabernacle wings closed, showing the figures of Saint John the Baptist and Mary Magdalen in gold relief with enamel. Note the similarity to the *enseigne* in the Bartolommeo Veneto portrait, plate 48.

Colorplate 17

Colorplate 16

Colorplate 18

Piero della Francesca, Botticelli, Lorenzo di Credi, Michelozzo, Donatello, Verrocchio, as well as, by implication, his greatest pupil, Leonardo da Vinci—all these renowned fifteenth-century artists were either actively engaged in making jewelry or involved in some way in its design. We might also add the names of artists whom we do not know for certain to have been apprenticed but who have depicted jewels in a manner clearly indicating professional interest. Vittore Carpaccio (at work 1490–1523) and Carlo Crivelli (1430?–1494), for instance, have rendered jewels in their paintings with a delicacy and precision bordering on trompe l'oeil. At least one other instance deserves mention. Francesco Raibolini (1450?–1517), called Francia,

50.
In a portrait by Piero della Francesca (1420?–1492), the Duchess of Urbino, Battista Sforza, wears a headdress characteristic of her time, but the "dog collar" with its great pearls, the strand of beads and the massive oval pendant might in combination have been worn by a belle of the Edwardian era. Italian, fifteenth century. Uffizi Gallery, Florence

51.
Domenico Ghirlandaio's portrait of the beautiful Giovanna Tornabuoni (b. 1468) includes exquisitely precise renderings of two marvelous jewels: the gem-and-pearl pendant at Giovanna's bosom and the fantastic brooch on the back shelf. Italian, 1488. Thyssen-Bornemisza Collection, Lugano, Switzerland

52.
A pair of ingenious, highly decorative whistles sketched by Albrecht Dürer. One is evidently a pendant; the other, at top, lacking a suspension ring, may have been intended as a finger ring. German, sixteenth century. British Museum, London

53.
An enchanting design for a pendant done by Hans Holbein the Younger when he lived in England. The inscription reads *Well laydi well.* English, 1532–43. British Museum, London

54.
Holbein's Dantesque miniature on paper of Lot and his family fleeing the destruction of Sodom was translated into a jewel (see plate 57), very likely the exact size of this original drawing—2 inches (5.1 cm.) in diameter. English, 1532–40. British Museum, London

50

ARS VTINAM MORES
ANIMVM QVE EFFINGERE
POSSES PVLCHRIOR IN TER
RIS NVLLA TABELLA FORET
MCCCCLXXXVIII

51

52

53

SLOT·GEN·19

54

is known to have signed his paintings *Opus Franciae Aurificis*, meaning "The work of Francia the goldsmith." This loyalty to the calling adds credence to the tradition that Francia fashioned a jewel so admired that he was asked to depict it in his great Felicini altarpiece for the church of Santa Maria della Misericordia in Bologna. The actual jewel has vanished; the painted counterpart remains.

The most eminent northern equivalents of the Italian artist-jewelers were the German painters Albrecht Dürer (1471–1528) and Hans Holbein the Younger (1497?–1543). Dürer, the son and pupil of a goldsmith, has left a number of imaginative sculptural designs (plate 52). Holbein designed superb jewels (plates 53 and 54) and also on occasion, like Francia, recorded them in his painting (plate 57).

It is probably not an exaggeration to say that at no other time in history, except perhaps in ancient Greece, was such a galaxy of talent at work on jewelry. Sadly, we have to add the corollary that none of the surviving jewels can be attributed with certainty to any of the great names enumerated here. The usual causes, including loss and accident, may be assumed to be largely responsible, though the more valuable jewels were perhaps most vulnerable to greed and theft. Cellini again is a witness: during the siege of Rome in 1527, he was

55 & 56.
A perfect epitome of the art and craft of Renaissance jewelry, this gold reliquary pendant decorated with enamel and pearls is equally beautiful on both faces. The front depicts the Annunciation in gold relief, while the reverse displays glowing pierced strapwork evocative of the rose windows of Gothic cathedrals. Italian, second half of the fifteenth century. Metropolitan Museum of Art, New York, gift of J. Pierpont Morgan, 1917

55

56

57.
A Lady of the Cromwell Family, by Hans Holbein the Younger. The jewel on the lady's breast was designed by Holbein (see plate 54) and probably made by his close friend the goldsmith Hans van der Goes of Antwerp (known in England variously as Hans of Antwerp, John of Antwerp and John Anwarpe), a jeweler to King Henry VIII. Date of the portrait, c. 1535–40. Toledo Museum of Art, Toledo, Ohio, gift of Edward Drummond Libbey

commissioned by Pope Clement VII (Giulio de' Medici) to remove all the gems from the jewels in the Apostolic Camera and melt the gold settings; the bullion thus obtained weighed 200 pounds (90.6 kg.). The Maecenases of the Renaissance could be ruthless destroyers as well as great builders. A mere sixteen years later, in 1543, Clement's successor, Paul III (Alessandro Farnese), issued a similar order. It happened that while the foundations of Saint Peter's Basilica were being extended, the tombs of two Roman empresses were discovered, brimful of splendid jewels. Paul ordered the gems removed and had them transferred to a new papal tiara—destined to be looted a few centuries later by Napoleon Bonaparte.

Cellini expressed no objections to the task he was required to carry out, perhaps because he believed that he and his contemporaries could surpass the achievements of the past. In some respects at least, the presumption was justified. The jewelers of the sixteenth century were marvelous technicians, capable of meeting every demand made of them. The characteristic jewel of the Renaissance is the pendant, in a bewildering variety of forms and subjects (colorplates 15 and 17–21; plates 53, 55, 56, 58–63, 67 and 68). No stylistic generalization is possible; each example, often dense with symbolism and imagery, must be considered individually. We cannot always, as their contemporaries could, extract to the full the significance of these "jewels *à clef*," but their beauty is self-evident, as is the technical virtuosity of

58

59

58.
A heart-shaped devotional pendant decorated in *verre églomisé*. The gold glinting beneath the glass cover casts a dramatic light on the scene of Christ at Gethsemane. Spanish or Italian, late sixteenth century. Smithsonian Institution, National Collection of Fine Arts, gift of John Gellatly

59.
A reliquary cross of enameled gold with geometrically faceted slabs of rock crystal framed by voluted architectural strapwork. German, dated 1586. Metropolitan Museum of Art, New York, gift of J. Pierpont Morgan, 1917

60 & 61.
The front of a *commesso* pendant, with an allegorical figure of Prudence in wrought gold. The head and hands are carved of white chalcedony, the snake is enamel, the mirror is a diamond and the frame has rubies and emeralds. The reverse, of different workmanship, depicts Diana the Huntress in translucent enamel, after a design by the celebrated French jeweler-engraver Étienne Delaune (1518–1595). The front is probably Italian in origin; the reverse is French, School of Fontainebleau. Sixteenth century. Metropolitan Museum of Art, New York, gift of J. Pierpont Morgan, 1917

62.
A pendant with a glowing head of Medusa beautifully sculptured in chalcedony. The stylized gold surround, of cutout scrolls with gems in high collets, is decorated with enamel and a pearl. Italian, probably Milan, c. 1570. National Gallery of Art, Washington, D.C., Widener Collection

63.
An enameled pictorial pendant in a plain frame, with the title *Solomon Turns to Idolatry*. Enameling became almost entirely a painter's medium during the late Renaissance, and other decorative elements were subordinated or excluded altogether. French, Limoges, sixteenth century. Walters Art Gallery, Baltimore

60

61

62

63

their makers. The complexity and variety of their forms offer scholars an occasional clue to national origin or date of execution. What matters most, however, to the student and collector of jewelry is that these triumphs of High and late Renaissance art combine the mediums and styles of the past with styles, substances and techniques of their own. Foremost among the techniques must be ranked further refinements of enamel decoration, such as *verre églomisé* (plate 58) and *émail en résille sur verre*. The first of these was a technique practiced in antiquity of first painting designs on the reverse of glass plaques and then applying to the designs a ground of gold or silver leaf or foil. The second consisted of fusing a particularly delicate enamel to an engraved glass surface—a technique so demanding that it was practiced only occasionally even then and has rarely been attempted since.

By the late Renaissance, jewels had become as much fashion accessories as portable works of art and objects of devotion. Thus came

64.
A page from a book of jewelry patterns brought out by René Boyvin (1530–1598), of Angers, reflecting the influence of the School of Fontainebleau. Devoted primarily to finger rings, the page also includes designs suitable for neck chains or bracelets. The inscription at bottom gives the name of the engraver, Paul de la Houve. French, sixteenth century. Cooper-Hewitt Museum Library

65.
In 1576 Etienne Delaune, known as Stephanus, did an engraving of what may well have been his own workshop in Strasbourg. These northern goldsmiths worked in surroundings more prosaic than those of their southern counterparts (see plate 47). The man at right may be firing precisely such a delicate enameled jewel as that in plate 61. Bibliothèque des Arts Décoratifs, Paris, Collection Maciet

about the rise, chiefly in France and Germany, of professional designers whose task it was to create and publish patterns for the use of jewelers who were essentially craftsmen rather than artists. Earlier, such craftsmen had turned for their models to books of hours, hymnals and missals—sources not always readily accessible. Jewelry patterns now became widely available through the development of intaglio engravings on paper. Credit for originating such engraved prints has been given to the fifteenth-century Florentine goldsmith Maso Finiguerra, who is said to have evolved it from *niello*, a technique of metal ornamentation.

During the sixteenth century, artists of great merit from different lands contributed to this process of popularizing jewelry designs. We must name at least a few: Jean Duvet, Étienne Delaune (plates 61 and 65), Jacques-Androuet Du Cerceau, René Boyvin (plate 64), Hans Brosamer, Virgil Solis, Daniel Mignot, Erasmus Hornick, Pierre Woeiriot and Matthias Zundt. Their designs, conceived as practical models for craftsmen-jewelers, are now esteemed as works of art on their own merits. Faithful reflections of the taste and stylistic currents of an epoch, they are of major interest to the student and collector.

Despite this internationalization of patterns, certain regional characteristics remained strongly entrenched. In Germany, for instance, gold chains were considered not merely useful for the suspension of pendants but important in themselves. At times, this was carried to extremes. One painting, for example, shows a German princess all but

66.
The German painter Hans Krell (at work c. 1522–86) portrayed Princess Emilia of Saxony (1516–1591) in her betrothal finery, as indicated by the symbolic joined hands embroidered on her bodice and repeated in the links of the central necklace. Crescent-shaped aglets ornament the ribbon bows of the hat. (Formerly thought to be a portrait of his wife by Lucas Cranach the Elder.) German, sixteenth century. Walker Art Gallery, Liverpool

overburdened with chains, one of which has links almost the size of bracelets (plate 66). Perhaps this sort of display betrays a lingering medievalism; certainly it is in marked contrast to the sophistication of the jewelry shown in a detail from a portrait by an Italian artist of the period (plate 67).

Just as the Age of Gold took place in antiquity, and the Age of the Diamond would appear in the future, so the Age of the Pearl occurred during the Renaissance. Pearls are everywhere: as neck ropes (plate 69); as part of the attire of both men and women; as elements of jewels (plates 50, 51 and 68; colorplate 15). Few fine pendants lacked the final touch of a pearl drop (plates 60–62; colorplates 17–19), or of several such drops (plate 53; colorplates 15 and 20). Pearls of the type now called baroque (that is, irregularly shaped) played a para-

67.
Detail from *A Lady as Lucretia*, painted by Lorenzo Lotto (c. 1480–c. 1556). The splendidly sculptural pendant on swags of supple link chains exemplifies the ultimate refinement in Renaissance luxury and elegance. Italian, sixteenth century. National Gallery, London

mount role in such figural jewels as a splendid Triton pendant (colorplate 21) in which the merman's torso and tail appears as if sheathed in a nacreous cuirass. If a pearl of proper shape and size was not readily available, the desired effect—as of a sculptural mass of white marble—might be obtained by the use of white *émail en ronde bosse* instead (colorplate 20).

67

Mythological themes appeared in Renaissance jewelry (plate 62; colorplates 15, 20 and 21), as did evocations of classical history (plate 70), allegories (plate 60) and portraits of crowned heads (colorplate 18). There were religious themes as well. Hints of the Reformation are evident in the use of episodes from the Old Testament, as in a Limoges plaque of Solomon worshipping idols, a transparent allusion to papal domination (plate 63); and the fervor of the Counter-Reformation is apparent in such increasingly subtle mystical themes as that of the Sacred Heart, a particular favorite among Spanish jewelers, as implied in a heart-shaped pendant of Christ in the Garden of Gethsemane (plate 58).

The wealth, power and spiritual prestige of Renaissance Spain led to the widespread adoption of dress of dark and severe Spanish magnificence, almost Byzantine in its abhorrence of even partial nudity

68.
A necklace or collar of gold, enamel, diamonds and pearls, with three pendants. Designed to be worn from shoulder to shoulder, it may have been ordered as a wedding gift: paired hands and kissing birds appear in the central pendant and the two end elements. German, possibly Augsburg, early seventeenth century. Walters Art Gallery, Baltimore

69.
A portrait by Juan Pantoja de la Cruz (1551–1608) of Elisabeth de Valois, third wife of Philip II of Spain. The ovoid pearl depending behind her left ear is the famed La Peregrina (The Wanderer), which has been included in portraits of the queens of Spain ever since its discovery in Panama in about 1550 by a slave for whom it won freedom. Spanish, sixteenth century. Prado, Madrid

and its passion for richness. The portrait of Elisabeth de Valois (1545–1568), daughter of Henry II of France and third queen of Philip II of Spain (1527–1598), supplies an ideal example (plate 69). On her high-necked gown—for décolletage was a thing of the past—the young queen wears a jeweled *carcanet* (a close-fitting collar); a matching girdle accents her long V-shaped bodice, and her skirt and sleeves are fastened with jeweled tags called *aglets*. In her right hand she holds the gem-encrusted gold marten's head that is attached to her real marten fur piece. Interestingly enough, a counterpart of this fashion accessory has been preserved (colorplate 22).

Colorplate 19.
A galleon pendant or *nef*—so called from the old French term for a vessel—with full rigging and a "crew" of three, fashioned of gold with enamel, crystal, rubies and a pearl. In an age of maritime exploration and increased trade with the Far East, the ship was a favorite motif for jewel designs. German, late sixteenth century. Metropolitan Museum of Art, New York, Michael Friedsam Collection, 1931

Colorplate 20.
Two pendants with representations of animals, a much-favored theme of the late Renaissance. Opaque white enamel *en ronde bosse* is used for the animal and human figures; the pearl drops serve to "cool" the high colors of the enameled gold set with rubies, emeralds and diamonds. Metropolitan Museum of Art, New York. *Left*: A rider in Roman armor mounted on a camel. German, c. 1600. Bequest of Michael Friedsam, 1932. *Right*: *Rape of Europa*. Italian or German, late sixteenth–early seventeenth century. Gift of George Blumenthal, 1941

COLORPLATE 19

COLORPLATE 20

Colorplate 21

Colorplate 21.
A baroque pearl, its naturally uneven surface suggesting the rippling muscles of an athletic torso, has been combined with gold, enamel, diamonds and rubies to fashion this great Triton pendant. Italian or French, late sixteenth century. Smithsonian Institution, National Collection of Fine Arts, gift of John Gellatly

Colorplate 22.
A lifesize head of a marten, of wrought gold sumptuously ornamented with enamel and encrusted with pearls and faceted rubies in high box collets. It was one of the most luxurious refinements of late Renaissance fashion to attach such a jeweled artifact to a real fur piece, as shown in the portrait of the Queen of Spain in plate 69. Italian, probably Venetian, 1550–60. Walters Art Gallery, Baltimore

Colorplate 22

70.
A *commesso* ring composed of a cameo profile of Alexander the Great in opaque turquoise blue glass with tumbling hair of tooled gold in an enameled frame. Possibly Italian, sixteenth century. Metropolitan Museum of Art, New York, Rogers Fund, 1910

71.
A necklace of stylized bows reflecting the severe and delicate taste prevalent at the end of the seventeenth century. It is made of gold almost entirely covered with black and white enamel and set with diamonds, a pearl and a pear-shaped cabochon sapphire. French, late seventeenth century. Victoria and Albert Museum, London

With the end of the sixteenth century and the start of the seventeenth, there began to develop in jewelry what may be regarded as an increase in the influence of personal taste. It was then that jewels, though still essentially miniature works of art, began to conform more closely to the wearer's personality than to the maker's. Significantly, the locket, with its hint of something secret concealed inside, now often replaced the purely ornamental pendant. Decoration, too, began to undergo a notable change, with emphasis on stylized floral forms and imaginative arabesques (see plate 61, page 75). Increasingly, jewels seem to have been created primarily for personal delectation, and they repay close examination, especially with the aid of a magnifying glass.

Another important fashion change was the supplanting of the *enseigne* by the *aigrette*, originally a tuft of feathers held in place on the cap by a brooch or clasp but eventually transmuted into a jewel in the form of a stylized spray of mounted gems. Earrings, too, took on an importance they had not enjoyed since antiquity. Widely favored was the *girandole*, consisting of a central ornament from which depended three movable drops, either pearls or gems. Perhaps the most original contribution to the repertory of personal jewelry in the seventeenth century was the introduction of stylized bows, doubtless inspired by the knots of silk ribbons used in profusion on the costume of the time. Many such knots had been tipped with jeweled aglets, and it was a logical step to transform the entire element into a jewel (plate 71)—as had been done for the aigrette.

Brooches in the shape of ribbon bows are known as Sévigné brooches, named after that great lady of the era of Louis XIV, the Marquise de Sévigné (1626–1696), whose letters are acknowledged today as one of the glories of French literature. Both girandole earrings and Sévigné brooches were worn throughout the eighteenth century, so it is often forgotten that they originated considerably earlier. The same may be said of the use of diamonds in jewels; that, too, became more common in the seventeenth century, although the Age of the Diamond as such had yet to begin. Pearls in the seventeenth century were used as lavishly as ever—and even more imaginatively. Tear-shaped or pear-shaped, they served as ear drops and as hat ornaments; they bespangled lace ruffs and satin skirts. With a more delicate taste coming into vogue, a single row of especially large, perfectly spherical pearls, simply tied at the back with a velvet ribbon, was as dearly prized as any richly encrusted carcanet. A lady's hair, worn loosely in shoulder-length ringlets, was interspersed with strands of pearls; looped swags, or coils, of pearls closely followed the return to low décolletage for formal attire, going on to outline the pointed bodice and even reaching to the ground along the parted folds of the overskirt. Indeed, wherever we look, softly glowing pearls cast a lunar luster on that age of transition between the sunset of the Renaissance and the dawn of modern times.

5 The Age of the Diamond

The eighteenth century has had numerous appellations bestowed upon it: the Age of Reason, of Enlightenment, of Elegance, of Revolution. Yet it surely deserves one more, for as we have already suggested, it was also the Age of the Diamond.

Diamonds had long been known and used. By the seventeenth century, massive gems of one sort or another set in high collets (metal bands) already formed an important part of royal and other jewelry of unusual richness. This increased use of diamonds indicated the paramount role precious stones would ultimately play in European jewelry as a result of the maturing of a process believed to date back to the fourteenth century, when lapidaries (probably in Paris) first undertook to improve the natural look of the diamond.

At first, this stone had been used chiefly in its basic crystalline form of an octahedron (two pyramids with a joint base). Eventually, early lapidaries had learned how to halve the octahedron at the base, a step apparently taken for economic rather than optical reasons, since knowledge of the unique refractive quality of the diamond was still a long way off. Next had come the fourteenth-century development whereby lapidaries sliced off the apex of the pyramids, leaving a flat surface called the *table*, a technique that remained in use for centuries. Yet even with this improvement, the stones could still hardly be differentiated from slabs of rock crystal, and they were not highly prized. Accordingly, it was decided that they needed color: thus the settings were often lined with tinted foil that would impart a shading to the diamond. Such a lining might even be black, so that a table-cut diamond with a black background looked somewhat like a slice of jet. Benvenuto Cellini in the sixteenth century speaks with pride of his own skill in the delicate art of tinting gems this way, and the practice was continued in isolated instances even into the eighteenth century.

Colorplate 23.
A badge of the Order of the Golden Fleece made in 1765 for the Bavarian elector Maximilian III Joseph by the Munich court jeweler Johann Staff. One of the very few such jewels to have survived, it is a splendid example of the delicate coloring found in eighteenth-century jewelry, with the luminous tints of its pink brilliants softening the adamantine glitter of the white ones. The *pavé* setting is of gold. Schatzkammer der Residenz, Munich

One reason for the neglect of diamonds, apart from the fact that their possibilities were not yet understood, was their rarity. Cutters were afforded little opportunity to experiment. The situation changed with the opening up to the West of the celebrated Golconda diamond mines in India at the beginning of the seventeenth century and the discovery of great new fields in Brazil about a hundred years later.

In the mid-seventeenth century the *rose cut* was developed in Holland, by which the pyramidal form of the diamond was given a dome shape provided with at first sixteen and eventually twenty-four facets —the base, now circular, remaining flat. In the designs of great seventeenth-century specialists—those of Gilles Légaré, master jeweler of Louis XIV, for instance—twin versions of a design for a gemmed jewel are frequently offered, one employing the now old-fashioned table-cut gems, the other those of the newer rose cut. Rose-cut stones are shown in plate 72.

Rose-cut diamonds refracted light in flashing sparks, providing an effect far livelier than anything previously known. Around the beginning of the eighteenth century a still more complex cut, the *brilliant*, was evolved by the Venetian lapidary Vicenzo Peruzzi. Peruzzi's achievement might be called scientific rather than artistic; nevertheless, it affected jewelry more profoundly than the artistic currents of the age. This is easily understood if we recall that gems earlier had been simply one of several elements in the composition of a jewel, on a par, for instance, with enameling and pearls. But a truly fine brilliant-cut diamond pulsates with prismatic radiance, glitters with an almost living glow. No longer could such a gem be regarded as subordinate in a design.

There are two essential differences between the rose cut and the brilliant cut. The base of the rose cut is flat, whereas the base of the brilliant is a truncated, upside-down pyramid, called the *pavilion*. And the upper surface of the rose cut rises to a point, whereas the brilliant is polished flat. In a brilliant-cut diamond, the area between the upper and lower surfaces acts as a kind of reservoir for light rays, which are reflected and re-reflected endlessly by the facetings in the *girdle* (the widest part) of the stone. Thus the brilliant cut releases the iridescent fire at the heart of the diamond—and so, for good reason, diamonds became the most treasured of all gems, the prizes for which dynasties and reigning houses struggled with one another and which almost invariably changed ownership as a result of wars and revolutions.

Sometimes the diamonds disappeared altogether, and today we must turn to chronicles, inventories and portraits for a record of many of the most dazzling examples. Vanished long since, for instance, is the now-legendary badge of the Order of the Golden Fleece made for Louis XV of France. This famous jewel consisted of some of the largest and finest diamonds in royal possession. Combined with the diamonds was the stupendous, irregularly shaped ruby known as the Côte-de-Bretagne, which did survive the perils of the centuries and at present is in the Louvre. Also preserved in national treasuries are a few magnificent Golden Fleece badges that managed to survive intact. One, in the Palacio Nacional da Ajuda, near Lisbon, is a rainbow-hued marvel composed of huge, faultlessly limpid gems. Another splendid example, in the Residenzmuseum in Munich, belonged to the Bavarian elector Maximilian III Joseph, for the proud imperial electors of the Holy Roman Empire did not lag far behind the other European potentates in acquiring richly bejeweled insignia (colorplate 23). Queens and princesses could not wear the badge of a male order such as the Golden Fleece, but they appear to have compensated for this restriction with a splendid sort of "body jewelry." We have already taken note of Queen Charlotte's unusually large, gem-encrusted stomacher, for instance (plate 73), and plate 72 shows us a design for a corsage ornament of almost equal magnificence.

Such ostentatious creations were feasible only, of course, when the artist-jeweler could draw on a vast store of gems, as in a royal treasury. Clearly, the designing of other sorts of jewels was subject to practical considerations, and as a rule, only a limited number of gems was available. So diamonds were normally set much farther apart than in the great royal showpieces and were precut instead of being cut individually to follow a given design. It has been said that the eighteenth century loved light and lightness. This is basically true; but in jewelry, at least, such lightness was not always entirely a matter of choice. It was certainly by choice, however, that the light of the new brilliant-cut diamonds glittered from mounts of corresponding lightness, with silver often preferred to gold in the settings. The best jewelry of the eighteenth century is so timeless in style, so eminently wearable even today, that what little survives has remained largely in private hands. In comparison with, say, classical or Renaissance jewels, surprisingly few examples are to be found in museum collections in America (plates 74 and 75).

Relatively few examples have survived, as well, of what was perhaps the most original contribution of that age to the art of the jewel: jewels set with gem-cut glass rather than precious stones. *Antique paste*—or *French paste*, as it is often called, although production was not limited to France—is the term applied to these eighteenth-century jewels. To the modern mind, this may suggest counterfeiting, yet jewels of antique paste were not usually regarded as counterfeit but were valued for their own special beauty. True, not all of them were of equal merit, but it is no exaggeration to say that the best examples are often technically superior to jewelry set with precious stones and far more significant stylistically.

72.
A watercolor drawing of a design for a Sévigné bow corsage ornament, incorporating rose-cut diamonds, cabochon rubies, table-cut emeralds and graduated pearls. It would have rivaled the stomacher in plate 73 in splendor, if not quite in size. Italian, eighteenth century. Cooper-Hewitt Museum

73.
The impressive gem-encrusted stomacher worn by Queen Charlotte, wife of George III, in this state portrait appears more like an integral part of her costume than a separate item of jewelry. Stomachers were a favorite corsage ornament of the period. English, from the studio of Allan Ramsay, c. 1762. Detail. National Portrait Gallery, London

The reason for this is that the designer of paste jewelry, like the designer of royal ornaments, was unrestricted as to the number and form of the substances to be set in a given jewel. Still, shaping diamonds, the hardest of all gems, to fit a pattern was enormously expensive as well as arduous, and even a court jeweler had to make allowances for that. It was relatively easy to shape and fit glass "gems" into a pattern, although to set them was even more difficult than to set true gems: mounting and foiling, for instance, presented special problems.

74.
A graceful necklace of silver, gold and diamonds. The overlapping diamond chains form a delicate frame for the trellised lozenge motifs that carry the major stones. The clasp is modern. European, eighteenth century. Metropolitan Museum of Art, New York, gift of Ann Payne Blumenthal, 1958

75.
A brooch of diamonds set in silver and gold. A basket filled with stylized blooms and leafage was a seventeenth-century theme that remained popular throughout the eighteenth and nineteenth centuries. The larger stones are rose cut. English or French, second half of the eighteenth century. Cooper-Hewitt Museum, gift of Gertrude Sampson

74

75

76

76.
Two superb examples of strass paste: pendeloque earrings with their original hooks, and a Sévigné brooch with the original "saber" pin. The individually shaped stones are fitted to their silver mountings with faultless workmanship. French, first half of the eighteenth century. Private collection

77.
The use of precut circular paste "brilliants" and the preponderance of gold beading, in combination with a silver setting, mark this necklace as a late eighteenth-century jewel. The flat hooks are for the attachment of ribbon ties, a type of closure that preceded the modern hook. French, last quarter of the eighteenth century. Cleveland Museum of Art, gift of Mrs. Severance A. Millikin

77

Paste jewelry provided a medium for uninhibited expression of the stylistic ideals of the age. Only a king, perhaps, could have afforded shoe buckles of the sort shown in colorplate 24, lower left, had they been set with genuine diamonds. And certainly the nobleman or the wealthy bourgeois who might have owned these buckles (and even then such articles would have been far from cheap) would have had no grounds for attempting to deceive anyone. The paste gems had their own crystalline beauty, and were framed in gold or silver settings far more delicate than the settings of an earlier age. The Sévigné pin and *pendeloque* (single pendant) earrings seen in plate 76 seem almost totally devoid of any visible settings, and the individually matched paste gems outline the designs in ribands of light. As the eighteenth century wore on, such admirable workmanship became more and more rare, and in even the finest paste pieces, precut round "gems," sometimes erroneously called brilliants, were substituted for individually shaped and fitted elements of *strass* (colorplate 25 and plate 77).

Strass, a common synonym for paste jewels, derives from the surname of Georges-Frédéric Stras, or Strass (1701–1773), an Alsatian who became court jeweler to Louis XV and was renowned for his paste jewelry. He may or may not have invented a special jewelry-glass formula with a high percentage of lead, but either way, it says much for the prestige enjoyed by paste jewels that a leading jeweler of the age, official purveyor to the most elegant of French courts, should have taken such pride in the creation of what we would now consider costume jewelry, albeit of an exalted sort.

Although paste jewelry did not become generally fashionable until the eighteenth century, glass had been used in combination with precious or semiprecious stones as far back as the early Mediterranean cultures, as already noted (see the pectoral plaque in colorplate 3, page 17; and see plates 20 and 22, pages 33 and 37). Nor can there be much doubt that it was used throughout succeeding centuries, if sometimes with an intention to deceive. In the fourteenth century, a Paris ordinance specified that colored glass could not be combined with gems or set in precious metals "except for the use of the royal family, and of high church dignitaries." By the middle of the seventeenth century, such restrictions had evidently been lifted, for a certain Sieur d'Arce then became rich and famous with his imitations of precious gems. And as late as the first decades of the eighteenth century—that is, shortly before paste, under the impetus of Stras, came into wide use—gems of cut glass were still being used as in medieval times, set in precious metals and combined with pearls and enameling (plate 78).

The dominance of gem-set jewelry, whether the gems were genuine or not, has been attributed to a social phenomenon: the increase of what we now call night life, which in turn was a result of the development of more efficient candles. In any case, beautiful jewelry of

Colorplate 24.
Buckles, in their innumerable guises, were probably the predominant jewels of the eighteenth century.
Top left: Shoe buckle of emerald paste and silver. *Top right*: Hat buckle of cabochon amethyst and faceted diamond paste, mounted in silver. *Center*: Fichu buckle of foiled almandines and vermeil. *Bottom left*: Shoe buckle of faceted diamond paste, gold and silver. *Bottom right*: Shoe buckle of topaz paste and "brilliants."
All, French eighteenth century. Buckle at lower left, Cooper-Hewitt Museum, gift of Mrs. Max Farrand. All others, private collection

Colorplate 25.
Paste diamonds and amethysts set in gold alternate with trefoil motifs of the same gems in a formal necklace of the late Georgian era. English, c. 1790. Cooper-Hewitt Museum, gift of Mrs. William E. Strong

Colorplate 24

Colorplate 25

chased gold, embellished with pearls and painted enamels, continued to be produced, presumably for daytime wear. Some of this work, in keeping with the standards of the age, is of extraordinary grace and daintiness. The characteristic jewel of the time, however, was probably the buckle, begemmed or otherwise, in all its forms and variations. Whether singly for the hat (where it replaced the *enseigne* and the aigrette) and the belt, or in pairs for garters and shoes, the eighteenth-century buckle was ubiquitous and often exceedingly rich (colorplate 24). And if worn on a silk band encircling the throat, or on an armband as a bracelet, it became indeed a piece of traditional jewelry.

Many items in this category—rings, pendants, lockets, breastpins, bracelet clasps—were so made as to include some element of personal significance: a portrait, a lock of hair under glass, a cipher (plates 79 and 80), an inscription, a date. These precious mementos are often exquisite in workmanship, but their appeal today is minor, as is their decorative worth. They do little more than reflect, gracefully but perfunctorily, the stylistic idiom of the epoch (plate 80).

During the last half of the century jewelry inset with miniature medallions and plaques picturing classical subjects was widely worn (plate 81). Since ornaments of this kind had great appeal but were costly, they were soon commercialized, the best-known productions being those incorporating pseudocameos of a fine-grained mat stoneware created by the British master potter Josiah Wedgwood (1730–1795) and known as jasperware. The raised ornamentation of jasperware, in pure white, appears generally on a ground of the lovely tint still known as Wedgwood blue, although the ware was also made in other colors, particularly a soft sage green. The setting is usually of gold, but occasionally of faceted steel. The most famous as well as the most appealing combination is of the blue and white medallions framed in gold. Wedgwood jewelry was relatively low in cost because it was turned out by what then amounted to mass-production methods. It was one of the harbingers of the industrialization of jewelry to follow in the next century.

78.
The ancient practice of using colored glass "gems" was never entirely abandoned in the eighteenth century, even after the rise in fashion of colorless strass.

Left: An exceedingly delicate pair of Louis XV earrings of vermeil, with foiled pink paste and pearls. *Center*: A silver cross enameled in black and white, with foiled clear crystal oval pastes in gold filigree mountings and clusters of pearls at the center. *Right*: A silver cross with arms of tear-shaped amethyst pastes, pale green table-cut pastes at the center, pearls and black and white enameling on scrolls of silver wire.

French, earrings c. 1735, crosses late seventeenth–early eighteenth century. Private collection

79.
The dedication page of the *Dictionnaire de Chiffres et de Lettres Ornées*, an influential pattern book for ornamental monograms and lettering by Jean-Henri Pouget (d. 1769), published in 1767. The cipher of the Marquise de Marigny appears at right, surrounded by the Three Graces. She was the wife of a powerful minister, the brother of Madame de Pompadour. His patronage of the arts is symbolized by the objects shown below his own monogram (left, upheld by Eros). Cooper-Hewitt Museum Library

80.
An oval locket of paste, enamel, gold and silver, with bow and tangled cipher, reflects the trends set by Jean-Henri Pouget and other designers, who themselves were influenced by such contemporaries as Boucher, Greuze and Fragonard. French, c. 1770. Cooper-Hewitt Museum, gift of the Misses Hewitt from the collection of Mrs. Abram S. Hewitt

81.
A pendant of sardonyx cameo set in gold, with smaller cameos and carved gems in the cutout surround and with a pendent pearl. The piece is not a copy of a classical antique jewel but rather a clever pastiche, incorporating elements borrowed from antiquity—as was done during the Renaissance. French or English, mid-eighteenth century. Metropolitan Museum of Art, New York, gift of J. Pierpont Morgan, 1917

A MADAME
LA MARQUISE DE MARIGNY
Du Dieu des Arts j'osai suivre les traces,
J'ouvris mon âme au feu de ses rayons;
Mais jaurois effacé les traits de mes crayons
S'il ne m'étoit permis de les offrir aux Graces.

79

80

81

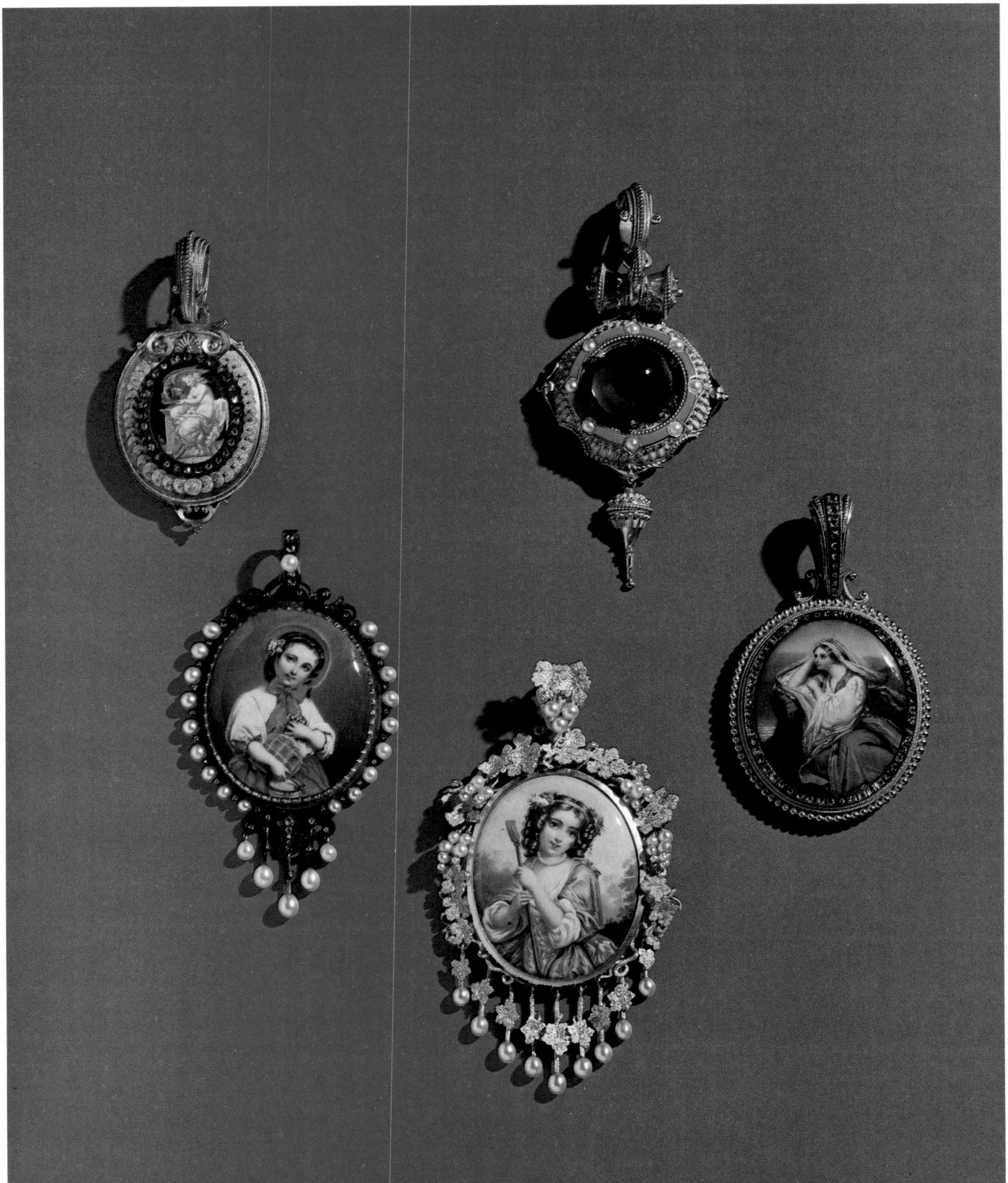

6 The Age of Eclecticism

"We still have one or two sculptors left, and perhaps three or four painters; jewelry still continues in a fair way, but the end is in sight, for no one will buy anything but diamonds anymore." Thus in 1776 the Comtesse de la Marck, a grandniece of Madame de Maintenon, expressed her misgivings about the future of jewelry to a royal correspondent, King Gustavus III of Sweden. Events were to prove her both right and wrong: diamonds continued to reign supreme, and as a result, jewelry as an art did suffer an almost total eclipse; yet the quantity, if not always the quality, of jewelry produced during the nineteenth century probably exceeded the output of all previous ages together. This was due to social changes that could hardly have been foreseen in 1776, and that brought with them not only shifts in taste but also shifts in the distribution of wealth.

The French Revolution, once it erupted, swept away aristocratic elegance and luxury in France—for a time. With the establishment of the Napoleonic empire, however, every effort was made to recapture them—and in the meantime the rival courts of London, Saint Petersburg and Vienna, and of other European monarchies, had never ceased to dazzle. At Napoleon's coronation, the new emperor could hardly do less than deck his person with an array of gems easily amounting to an imperial ransom. Similarly splendid ensembles were bestowed upon the reigning empress, as well as upon princesses in the Bonaparte family. The emphasis was now on large gems, set more simply yet more massively than had been customary under the Old Regime, when even the most splendid stones were likely to have been subordinated to an overall design rather than glorified for their own sakes. The effect now sought was not so much elegance as a revival of the magnificence of the Roman Empire. The diadem and tiara, neglected since the time of the Caesars, once again came back into fashion.

Colorplate 26.
A group of mid-nineteenth-century lockets and pendants reflecting a diversity of style and inspiration.

Clockwise from top right: An American locket, its central element a garnet carbuncle in the Greek tradition; two Swiss productions offering an interesting contrast between sophisticated simplicity (the locket at right center) and naive exuberance (the pendant below); a French medallion pendant with an oval frame echoing the subtle elegance of the late Renaissance; a French locket in the classical mode, with a miniature of Hebe pouring nectar for the Jovian eagle.

All pieces are of gold and enamel embellished with pearls or diamonds, or both. Cooper-Hewitt Museum, gifts from the Estate of and in memory of Mrs. Robert B. Noyes

In a similar neoclassical mood, large cameos were used in abundance—often combined with pearls and precious stones—in complex sets, or *parures*, that generally included coronal, comb, necklace, brooches and bracelets, and also a buckle for the belt that was a feature of the high-waisted feminine attire of the period. The craze for cameos, antique or not, was carried to such extremes that an elegant woman of the era sometimes appeared to be a walking *cabinet des médailles*.

But Napoleon's empire was short-lived, and a certain discretion reappeared during the Restoration that followed in France, as it did in much of the rest of Europe (plate 82), for financial reasons, among others. Less costly gems—amethysts, topazes, turquoises—came into use even for court wear, and less costly settings were devised; for instance, *cannetille*, a kind of lacelike gold filigree, replaced the more substantial and costly gold mounts (plate 83). Although believed to have originated in England, this new type of setting is known by the French word for the metallic floss used in needlework, an allusion to its thinness, which is not without a certain charm (colorplate 27).

82.
A delicate locket of gold, mother-of-pearl and glass exemplifies the neoclassicism of the late eighteenth century that remained in favor in Great Britain well into the nineteenth century. English, c. 1820. Cooper-Hewitt Museum, bequest of Katherine Strong Welman

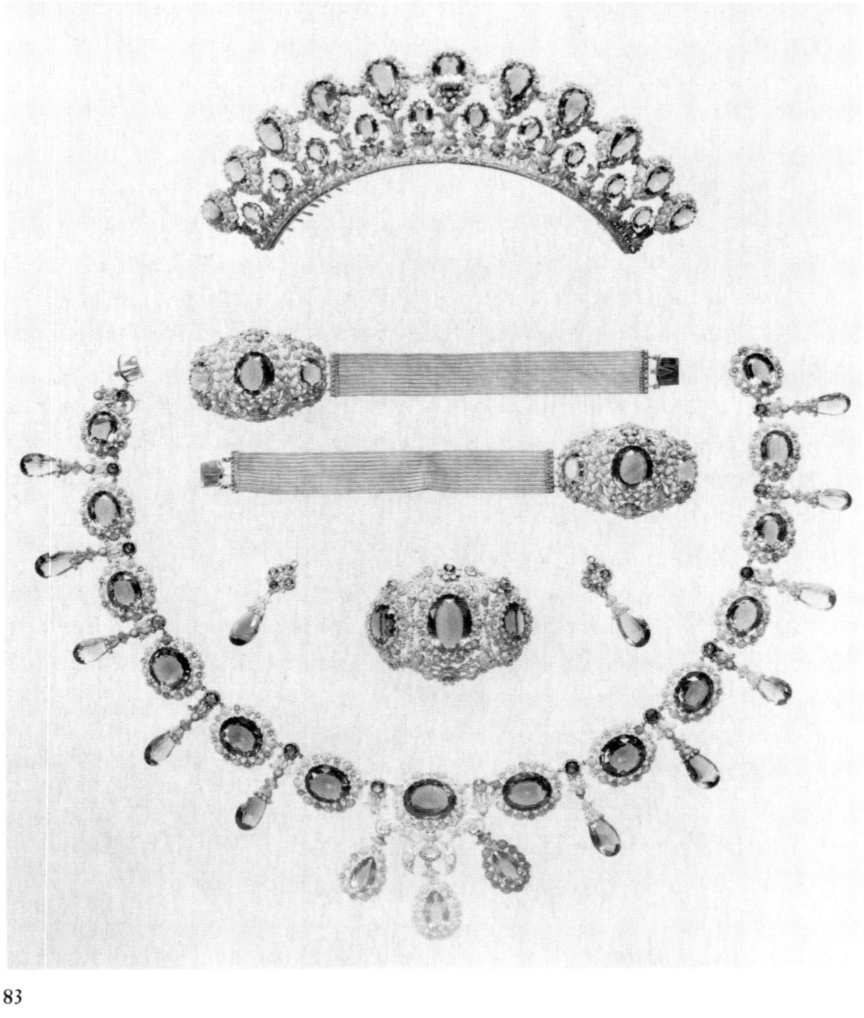

83

83.
A *grande parure* of amethysts mounted in cannetille gold, said to have belonged to a member of the Bonaparte family. The entire set—tiara, necklace, earrings, brooch and two bracelets—would have been suitable for court functions or other highly formal events; but individual items, except for the tiara and perhaps the necklace, could have been worn on less stately occasions. French or Italian, c. 1815–25. Metropolitan Museum of Art, New York, Michael Friedsam Collection, 1931

Colorplate 27.
A necklace and brooch from a parure (earrings and bracelet not shown) of souvenir jewelry brought back from Italy, typically featuring miniature views of ancient ruins and monuments—the Victorian equivalent of modern snapshots and color slides. The stone mosaic medallions are mounted in plain gold frames between motifs of cannetille gold. Italian, mid-nineteenth century. Cooper-Hewitt Museum, gift of Mrs. John Innes Kane, from the Estate of and in memory of her sister, Mrs. Samuel W. Bridgham

84.
Two examples of the remarkable early nineteenth-century peasant jewelry of Normandy and Brittany. *Left*: A pendant and slide, of gold with paste "brilliants." *Right*: A cross with flexible pendant, of silver and foiled crystal. Cooper-Hewitt Museum, gift of Mrs. Max Farrand (pendant and slide); private collection (cross)

The casting and stamping of jewelry metals was already general practice, particularly with the alloy called *pinchbeck*. Other imitations were *ruolz*, invented in 1841, and *chrysocale*, also developed in the mid-nineteenth century. With the further invention in 1852 of a mechanical process for mass-producing gem settings, the production of jewelry was turning into an industry and ceasing to be a craft. Nor did paste jewelry fail to fall victim to industrialization. The last examples of the now-lost art of making fine paste jewelry were produced in the early years of the nineteenth century in the French provinces of Normandy and Brittany (plate 84).

By midcentury and the accession of Napoleon III (1808–1873) in France, however, there was no lessening of a desire for opulent display; and if, with the return of relative social and economic stability, there had been a corresponding burst of artistic creativity, examples of truly great jewelry might have resulted, perhaps even to rival those of the Renaissance. The talent and technical skill were readily available, and so were the necessary precious materials. Unfortunately, there was a backward-looking tendency in much of Europe (plates 85, 86 and 87), and the directions of these looks depended on the arbiters of elegance. In France, none was more influential than Napoleon III's empress, Eugénie (1826–1920), born Eugenia María de Montijo de Guzmán, of a noble Spanish family. Imbued with strong religious and monarchic sentiments, the empress held in particular reverence the memory of Marie Antoinette, Louis XVI's queen, who had gone to the guillotine in 1793. As a result, a resurgence of interest in the Louis XVI style, now dubbed the Marie Antoinette style, swept the decorative arts, especially jewelry. Techniques as well as moods of the previous century were again in fashion—for example, the court jeweler Oscar Massin revived *tremblant*, the style of mounting jewels in which the elements, set on flexible stems, vibrated incessantly (plate 88). On the whole, however, the Marie Antoinette style merely recalled a vanished age without, as a rule, evoking its special grace. A notable exception should be mentioned: a magnificent brooch made for Empress Eugénie in 1853, incorporating a number of the famous stones once grouped in the badge of the Order of the Golden Fleece worn by Louis XV. Utterly simple, basically nothing more than a butterfly bow with tassels hung from a classical rosette, this greatest of the jewels of the Second Empire owes its impressiveness to the beauty of its huge gems and to the advantage taken of their unusual shape: the bow is composed of two juxtaposed wing-shaped diamonds of extraordinary size and limpidity.

The jewelers of the mid-nineteenth century were by no means copyists only, and a number of ingenious and pleasing innovations came into style. One was the *pavé* (cobblestone) setting, which did away with the distracting, spotty effect of individually mounted diamonds of small size, uniting them instead in a scintillating, unbroken expanse (plate 102—see page 118—offers an example of later date). *Pavé* setting was also used felicitously for pearls and turquoises (see frontispiece). The process was brought to its ultimate refinement in the "invisible" setting known as the *monture illusion*, also evolved by the court jeweler Massin, in which the metal mounts are indeed very nearly imperceptible. Such developments tempted designers away from stylized patterns and toward naturalistic renderings. One of the corsage ornaments made for Empress Eugénie attempted to render in diamonds the myriad florets of a spray of lilac, and a diadem of wild roses was conceived for Eugénie's contemporary, the beautiful and unfortunate Empress Elisabeth of Austria (1837–1898).

Much attention was lavished by nineteenth-century jewelers on ornaments to be worn on the head. Besides diadems and tiaras, combs were in high favor. A characteristic element of the jewelry of the period was a flexible fringe of streamers of diamonds in graduated sizes. Called *pampilles*, these diamond streamers, or tassels, were never more spectacularly beautiful than when placed at the rim of a comb, where, swaying with every move of the wearer, they glittered like a waterfall. Combs might also be complemented with a gold mesh, or netting, in the classical mode; hairpins and hatpins, though utilitarian, were sometimes richly decorated (plates 89 and 90 and colorplate 28).

The nineteenth-century fancier of jewelry was attracted also to handsome if at times somewhat stolid "archaeological" jewelry made

85.
A design for a gold and cabochon-gem brooch by the renowned French jeweler Alexis Falize (1811–1898) displays the eclecticism as well as the opulence of the Second Empire, with evident stylistic kinship to the American locket in colorplate 26. French, c. 1860. Cooper-Hewitt Museum, purchased in memory of Mrs. Gustav E. Kissel

86 & 87.
Renaissance-style jewels were in favor during the late nineteenth century. *Left*: A pendant of gold, enamel, rubies, sapphires and pearls, after a design by Hans Collaert (1540–1622), made by Pierret, of Rome and Florence, c. 1875–90. *Right*: a pendant-brooch of gold, rose-cut diamonds, garnets and glass, with a Madonna and Child in gold. Probably Italian, c. 1880. Cooper-Hewitt Museum, gift of Marian Hague (pendant) and gift of Eugene L. Garbáty (brooch)

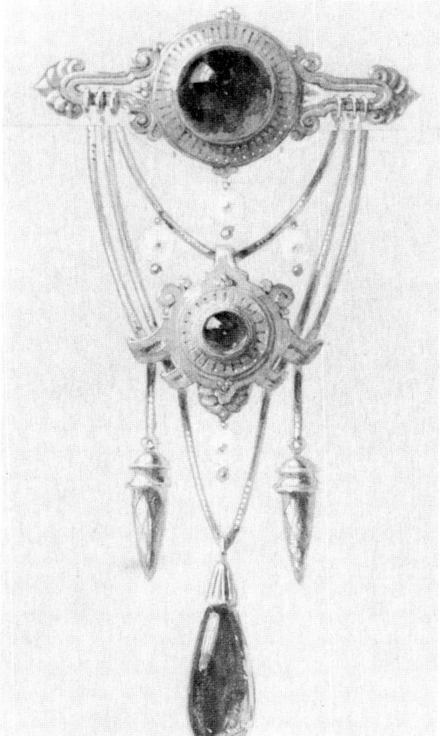

85

86

87

88.
A large brooch of gold and diamonds in *tremblant* mounting, in which each grain of the spray of wheat appears to shiver. The theme of ears of wheat, borrowed from classical antiquity, was a special favorite during the First Empire and was revived under the Second. French or English, nineteenth century. Cooper-Hewitt Museum, gift of Mrs. Boyd Hatch

88

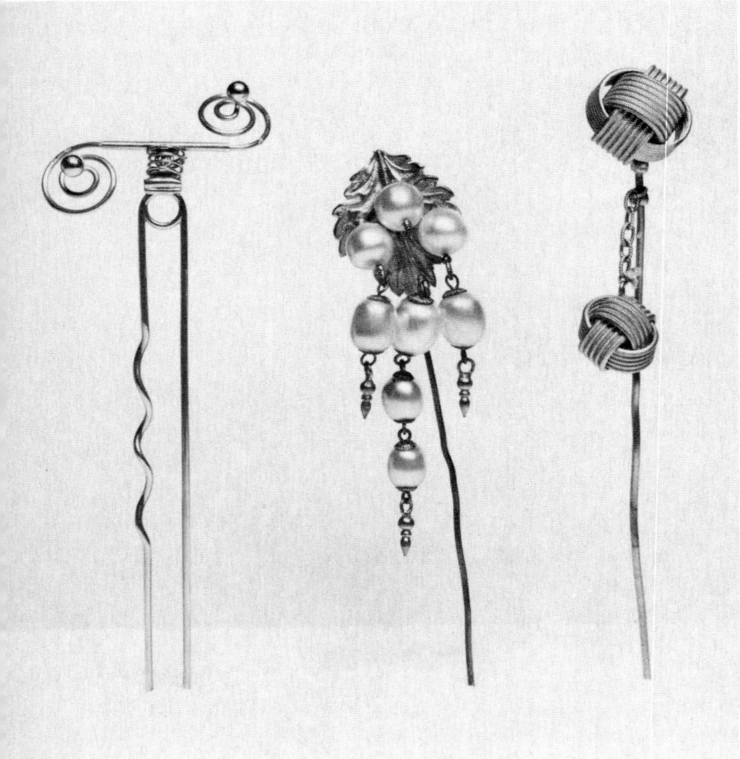

89

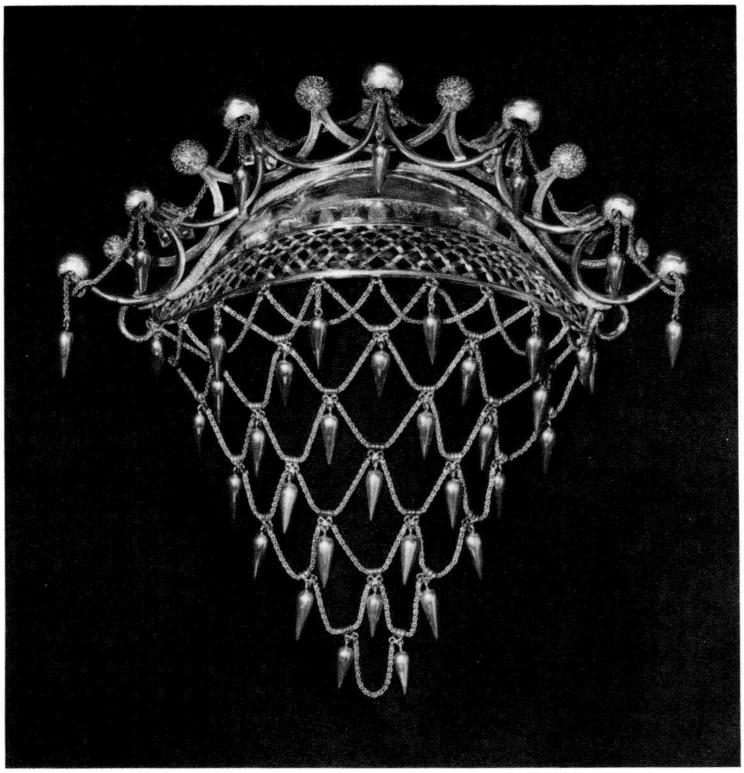

90

in imitation of Greek and Roman models. The best examples were a vast improvement over the mosaic jewelry then being turned out in the south of Italy for the tourist trade (colorplate 27). In a work entitled *Antique Jewelry and Its Revival*, the well-known nineteenth-century Italian scholar, collector and jeweler Alessandro Castellani (1824–1883) wrote of the archaeological movement: "In the first year of the present century [1801], a few attempts were made at Naples to copy exactly the ancient works in gold. The jeweler Sarno was the first promoter of this revival, which, helped by the advice of the Neapolitan archaeologists, and favored by the demand from abroad, prospered for a few years; and it is not easy to give any good reason for its gradual decay and dissolution. Afterwards, the artists who composed the school began to restore the gold ornaments found at Pompeii and Herculaneum, and applied their knowledge also to produce forgeries of them. They so wonderfully succeeded in this last reprehensible branch of industry that Naples became noted for such falsifications. So cleverly were they done, with the use of artificial color, and acids, and gold solutions, that it was nearly impossible for anyone not having a long practice in jewelry and a knowledge of archaeology to distinguish whether they were truly ancient or not."

It was then, Castellani goes on to say, that his own father (later also his master in the art), the Roman jeweler Fortunato Pio Castellani (1793–1865), decided that such copies should indeed be produced and sold, not as forgeries but as honest reproductions of masterpieces of the past. Still another factor was involved: the elder Castellani was interested in the scientific aspects of the subject, in metallurgy as well as in design. His ambition was to reproduce the style of ancient jewelry, and also to rediscover the techniques used by the early Etruscan jewelers—a knowledge of which, he was convinced, must still be preserved somewhere in what had been the Etruscan homeland. Accordingly, he undertook a thorough search of the Italian countryside and eventually concluded that he had indeed discovered ancient Etruscan secrets in a village of the Umbrian Marches, Sant' Angelo in Vado, a remote district of the Apennines. Craftsmen from this region were set to work, using their ancestral methods, to copy with absolute fidelity the models of antiquity.

Fortunato Pio Castellani was motivated by the highest purpose, as a patriot as well as an artist and a craftsman. Much of Italy was then under Austrian domination, and he wished to remind the world of his country's past glories extending as far back as the very dawn of history. When he retired in 1851, his task was continued with similar dedication by Alessandro and another son, Augusto (1829–1914).

The copies of ancient jewels made by the Castellanis are indeed superlative displays of technical skill, and look astoundingly like the originals (colorplate 28). There has always been divergence of opinion as to whether the delicacy of Etruscan beadwork was truly duplicated,

89.
Three mid-nineteenth-century hair ornaments. *From left to right*: Hairpin, gold, American; hair ornament, gold plate and imitation pearls, American; cap ornament, gold, French. Cooper-Hewitt Museum: bequest of Mrs. John Innes Kane (hairpin); gift of Mrs. Charles S. Fairchild (hair ornament); gift of the Misses Schuyler (cap ornament)

90.
Mid-nineteenth-century ornamental comb with chignon netting of gold with tortoiseshell, possibly German. Cooper-Hewitt Museum, bequest of Sarah Cooper Hewitt

Colorplate 28.
About the time Edgar Allan Poe was writing his exquisite lines on "the glory that was Greece and the grandeur that was Rome," the great nineteenth-century Italian jeweler Fortunato Pio Castellani was paying similar homage through his admirable copies of antique jewels, an endeavor later carried on by his two sons. All examples here are signed with their cipher, two capital C's linked back to back.

Clockwise from top left: A pair of gold earrings, each with the figure of a siren playing the lyre suspended from a classical rosette; a hair ornament in the form of a gold caduceus on an ivory staff; a gold brooch with an oval sapphire carved with the figures of the Roman matron Cornelia and her sons, the Gracchi; a necklace of gold, enamel, pearls and emeralds carved with miniature grotesque masks; a gold and emerald bracelet, after an ancient Scandinavian model, an example of the Castellani jewelry done in an antique style other than the classical. Cooper-Hewitt Museum, all purchased in memory of Annie Schermerhorn Kane and Susan Dwight Bliss, except earrings, gift of Eleanor Blodgett

but that in no way lessens the credit due this remarkable dynasty of Italian jewelers. One instance of their almost occult identification with the spirit of jewelers of ages past was furnished in a lecture delivered by Alessandro Castellani in Paris in 1860, before the Institute of France. He told how he and his brother Augusto had decided to include mosaic ornamentation on jewels made in the ancient Greek style even though, at the time, they knew of no examples of mosaic work in Greek jewelry. Then one day Alessandro discovered in the museum in Naples a superb Greek earring decorated with minute tessellations of precisely the sort he and Augusto had used.

Not all makers of archaeological jewelry were moved by the same impulses as the Castellanis. Such brilliant practitioners of the craft as Eugène Fontenay (1823–1887) in France or John Brogden (at work 1842–85) in England—as well as Castellani pupils such as Giacinto Melillo (1845–1915) and Carlo Giuliano (d. 1895)—were not content to subdue their own personalities and reproduce slavishly.

Although members of the Castellani family did reside for lengthy periods in England, where their productions were received with enthusiasm, they proudly continued to style themselves "of Rome." In contrast, Carlo Giuliano settled in London and in time became naturalized, so that he is now ranked as a British jeweler. Giuliano first opened a London workshop in 1861. By 1875, he had established an elegant boutique in Piccadilly that also served as an outlet for Castellani productions.

In addition to his archaeological jewelry, there are works bearing Giuliano's name that are outstanding for their variety and versatility. In addition to unusual interpretations from the antique, and also numerous pieces of Oriental inspiration (colorplate 29), one encounters again and again jewels mounted with table-cut gems set in high collets among foliated scrolls enameled in cool white and frosted further with a sprinkling of diamonds. If the descriptions sound not altogether unfamiliar, there is good reason: these creations, although patently original, often suggest the muted, somewhat melancholy grace of jewels of the seventeenth century. It was on the strength of this imaginative and highly personal style that Carlo Giuliano has been extolled as a designer of extraordinary talent. Recent research, however, seems to have established that while he was undoubtedly a skillful craftsman, his role was primarily as an entrepreneur, somewhat similar to that of the famous Russian court jeweler Peter Fabergé (1846–1920). This would leave Giuliano little time for either the designing or the execution of jewels. He had in fact a large staff, and watercolor drawings by his chief designer, Pasquale Novissimo, have been preserved. These drawings, intended to be shown to clients before the jewelry was made, display all the characteristics for which Giuliano jewels are renowned. Novissimo's drawings of archaeological jewelry also reveal special characteristics. One of these is the use of pointed petal shapes in rosettes rather than the rounded ones of the classical Greek models—a deviation Novissimo originated. It seems likely, therefore, that Giuliano's head designer also filled the demand for adaptations from the antique.

One of the most intriguing challenges of the study of nineteenth-century jewelry is to try to unearth the sources of apparent stylistic influences and to discover how such influences were combined (colorplate 26, page 98). Of the five pieces illustrated, a particularly interesting example is the exquisite Swiss locket with the figure of a seated woman looking out to sea. This jewel has a frame purely classical in mood and execution; the inner border of diamonds around the central miniature is clearly an echo of the eighteenth century; and the style of the miniature itself is obviously neoclassic. These characteristics alone prove that the locket, embodying as it does a medley of influences, could not have been produced earlier than the mid-nineteenth century. It is a typical hybrid of the time.

Jewelry trends of the nineteenth century were sometimes based on literary enthusiasms. The popularity of the so-called Ossianic lays of James Macpherson led to a renewal of interest in ancient Celtic ornamentation; and the immense vogue of Sir Walter Scott's historical novels inspired a craze for Gothic and romantic designs. A Parisian jeweler, François-Désiré Froment-Meurice (1802–1855), took to re-creating figural vignettes in relief that would have been better suited as illustrations for a medieval chronicle or a missal than to adorn jewels. Others, such as Augustus Pugin (1812–1852) in England, avoided similar incongruities by limiting themselves to use of the purely decorative medieval elements—trefoils (see the clasp bracelet in the frontispiece), ogives, semé patterns and the like. A highly popular ornament of the period was the *ferronnière*, a narrow band or chain with a central jeweled ornament, worn low over the brow and around the head. The term came from a painting in the Louvre, at the time attributed to Leonardo da Vinci and known as *La Belle Ferronnière* [*The blacksmith's beautiful wife*], in which the lady wears a jeweled fillet of this kind.

While such evocative items met with favor and were often made with great skill, they were neither faithful copies (like the "archaeological" jewelry) nor genuinely original artistic expressions. They represented what may have been a fundamental weakness of much nineteenth-century jewelry: the cultivation of virtuosity in place of creativity, plus an eagerness to memorialize in the form of jewelry significant events and outstanding figures of the age. Queen Victoria's fondness for all things Scottish brought on a flood of jewelry of Caledonian inspiration (see the plaid bracelet in the frontispiece). The opening of the Suez Canal, personally attended by Empress Eugénie, swamped the market with pseudo-Islamic jewelry. Finally, jewels

Colorplate 29.
Delicacy and imaginativeness characterize the jewels bearing the mark of Carlo Giuliano.

Top to bottom: A stylized brooch of gold, white enamel and pearls in the renowned "cool" style associated with the Giuliano name; a gold lovers' boat brooch, with figures enameled in full round and incrustations of diamonds, pearls, rubies, emeralds and sapphires, combining a subject of Hindu inspiration with execution worthy of the Renaissance; a fringed necklace of gold, enamel, pearls, cat's-eyes and ruby cabochons and beads, also evoking legendary India; a broad, geometrically decorated enameled gold bracelet as supple as an Oriental silk sash, inset with diamonds and cabochon rubies and bordered with half pearls.

English, London, late nineteenth century. Cooper-Hewitt Museum, purchased in memory of Annie Schermerhorn Kane and Susan Dwight Bliss

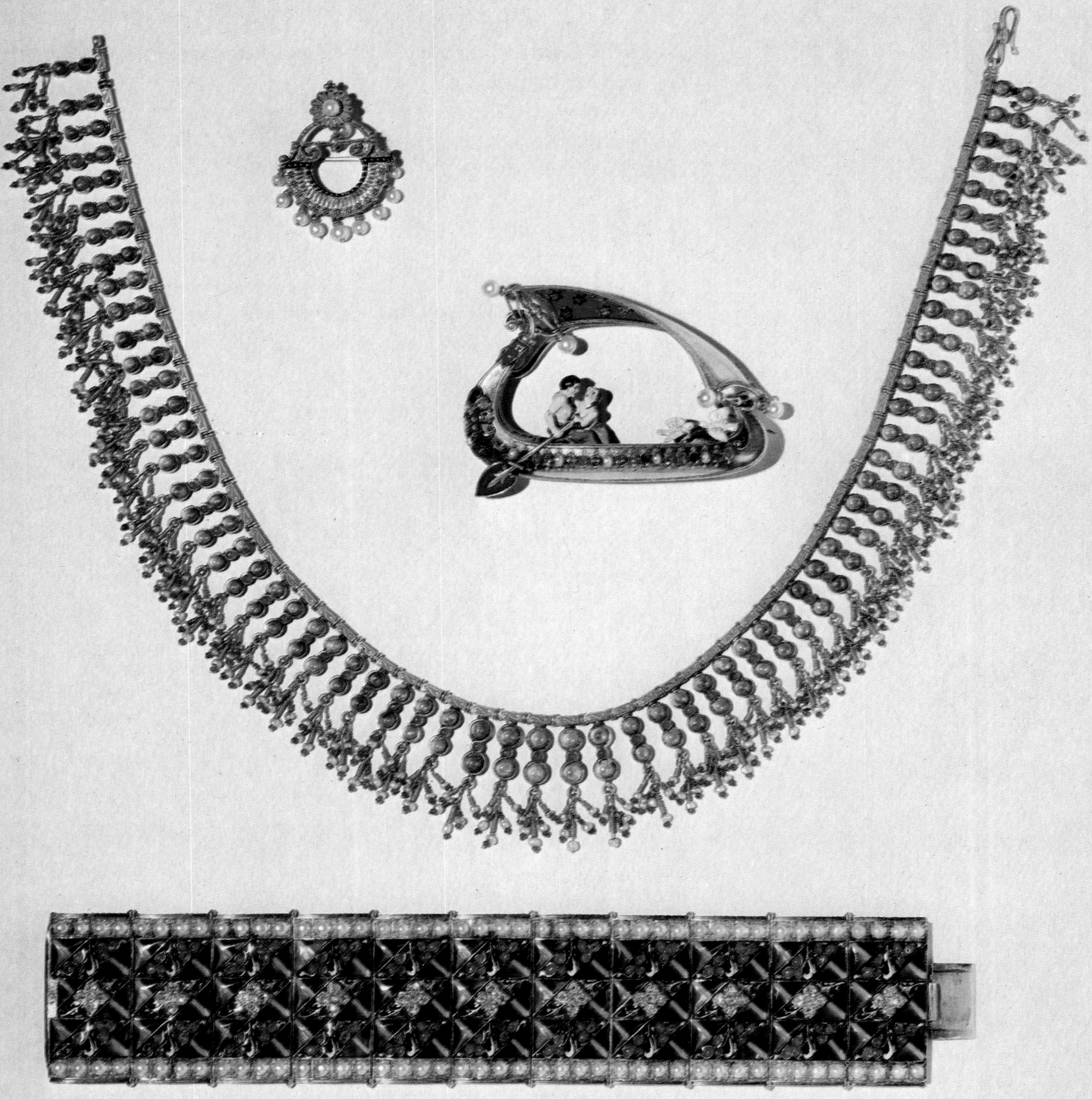

of Hindu design attracted renewed attention after Queen Victoria (1819–1901) was made Empress of India in 1876 (lovers' boat brooch and fringed necklace, colorplate 29), although as early as 1860, Alessandro Castellani had urged a serious study of the traditional Indian methods of goldsmithing and enameling, going so far as to say that the results of such a study might surpass in importance the rediscovery of Etruscan techniques.

Besides encompassing a multiplicity of themes, of which only a few can be mentioned here, jewelry began to be made from a number of substances hitherto rarely considered suitable for such purposes. We have noted the Italian tourist jewelry ornamented with mosaic (colorplate 27, page 101); lava from Vesuvius was also used. Shell cameos were another major Italian tourist jewelry form. Coral came into vogue in 1844, when the Duc d'Aumale (fifth son of Louis Philippe, king of the French) married Caroline de Bourbon, a daughter of the prince of Salerno of the Kingdom of the Two Sicilies (present-day Sicily and Naples), whence comes most of the world's precious coral. On this occasion, the bride was presented with remarkable coral jewelry. What might now be called ethnic elements also became popular: cairngorms and freshwater pearls from Scotland, bog

91.
In nineteenth-century mourning jewelry, the relationship between sentiment and ornament varied widely. An English brooch (*top*) of gold, seed pearls and paillettes has figural and braided hairwork, and is inscribed and dated 1837 on the reverse. An American locket of gold, onyx and rose-cut diamonds has a removable section in back containing a braid of hair under glass, and is inscribed and dated 1850. A Tiffany necklace of gold and onyx, made in Paris about 1880, is more elegant than mournful. Cooper-Hewitt Museum, gift of Mrs. Charles W. Lester (brooch) and gift from the Estate of and in memory of Mrs. Robert B. Noyes (locket and necklace)

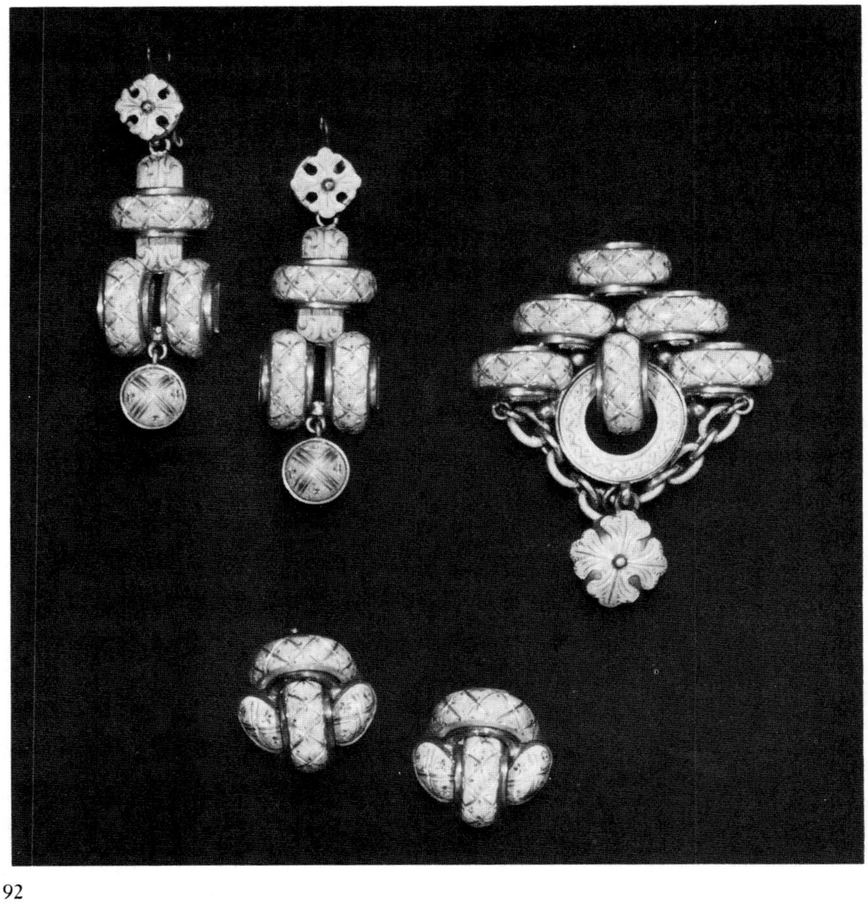

92.
An unusual example of aluminum jewelry, the then rare metal being combined with gold and finished to a soft, satiny luster. The set consists of a brooch, earrings (*upper left*) and cuff studs. German, second half of the nineteenth century. Cooper-Hewitt Museum, gift of Mrs. Gustav E. Kissel (brooch and earrings) and gift of Sarah Cooper Hewitt, Eleanor Garnier Hewitt and Mrs. James O. Green in memory of their father and mother, Mr. and Mrs. Abram S. Hewitt (cuff studs)

93.
In this bracelet of carved tortoiseshell, the motif of a smiling Bacchante, crowned with a vine wreath and flanked by a pair of Satyr heads in profile, reflects the neoclassicism of the Victorian era that remained popular in southern Italy long after the period ended. Naples, late nineteenth–early twentieth century. Cooper-Hewitt Museum, anonymous gift

oak and pyrite from Ireland. Also tiger claws; human hair (not in mere snippets as in the delicate memento mori of a previous generation, but sizable tresses braided, for instance, into a wide cuff bracelet); cut steel from Berlin and from Birmingham in England; assorted mineralogical specimens; various alloys and synthetic substances and a sort of hard rubber; jet, artificial as well as natural, and black onyx, for mourning as well as other purposes (plate 91); insects (scarabs and brightly colored beetles) and birds (heads of exquisite little hummers). Aluminum, then a scarce metal, was sometimes put to surprisingly felicitous use (plate 92). Ivory was carved in lacy patterns; seed pearls were mounted with a delicacy that resembled granulation. Tortoiseshell, an old favorite, was used in its natural state, highly polished and intricately carved (plate 93), or else was brightened with golden incrustations by the process known as *piqué* (plate 94), which had been brought to England by the French Huguenots in the seventeenth century, flourishing until the mid-eighteenth century. Piqué was revived in England about 1820 and declined about 1870, when it was cheapened by mass-production methods.

Queen Victoria continued to reign until her death in 1901, but the era that bears her name in Britain and elsewhere is generally understood to have ended considerably earlier, and the Edwardian era may be said to have begun before her eldest son succeeded her to the throne as Edward VII (1841–1910). Time had moved on, and a new generation had set a new mood. The jewelry in this new mood is not, one must admit, particularly distinguished, but much of it is at least pleasingly ornamental (plate 95). In France, a number of great

94

95

96

jewelry houses founded during the Second Empire continued to produce orthodox articles of top-quality jewelry, splendid in substance if disappointingly tame in design. A notable exception is perhaps the most truly beautiful jewel of the period: the famous "Russian" tiara of diamonds made for Alexandra of Denmark (1844–1925), who married the future Edward VII in 1863—a tiara crowning her, as it were, with a sheaf of glistening icicles from her native land. The simplicity and purity of its design are remarkable; neither Victorian nor Edwardian, it is truly timeless. Although it does not bear any specific national characteristic, it has been known from the start as the Russian tiara, because it was inspired by the ancient Russian headdress worn by women of all conditions there until the eighteenth century. However, it was only in the mid-nineteenth century, when several Russian empresses in turn elected to revive this national fashion in richly bejeweled, diadem-like versions, that this style attracted wide interest in Europe.

For less exalted individuals, "art" jewelry, with color and fantasy replacing sheer magnificence, was turned out by younger members of the Castellani and Giuliano families. If the fashions had begun to change, the principle remained the same; after all, it was Carlo

Giuliano who had first labeled himself an art jeweler. In the United States the designer most deserving of that label was certainly Louis Comfort Tiffany (1848–1933). He, however, designed but few pieces of jewelry, preferring to work instead as a painter and glassmaker, and had very little to do with the celebrated jewelry firm founded by his father, Charles Louis Tiffany (1812–1902). He cannot hence be held even indirectly responsible for some of the monstrosities that were made and sold by Tiffany & Company, among others. Few objects of this character have survived, having doubtless been broken up long ago and their massive gems reset. The chastening pictorial record survives (plate 96).

An interest in "sporting" jewelry also developed during the latter half of the century, featuring horses and horseshoes (often the one within the other), crops and whips, dogs, foxes, game birds, hunting horns and guns, anchors and sailboats, golf clubs, tennis rackets and balls and even the new "wheels," or bicycles. Such decorative paraphernalia, though made of precious substances, cannot be dignified by the name of jewelry—any more than the good-luck charms (four-leaf clovers, horseshoes, wishbones and the like) that became an enduring fad.

About 1900, one art critic stated categorically that for some thirty years it had been impossible to find contemporary jewelry "endowed with any artistic merit whatever." But even as this was being written, the situation had already begun to change. A powerful new art current, known as Art Nouveau and seeking to combine the best of East and West, made itself felt in the world of jewelry. Strongly influenced by the asymmetry of Japanese art, which had already inspired such painters as Manet, Monet, Whistler, Toulouse-Lautrec and Gauguin, it provided jewelers with an entirely new choice of subjects and a correspondingly extended range of textures and materials.

The career of Art Nouveau jewelry was short-lived. Scarcely encountered before 1895, by the time of the Paris Exposition of 1900 it was at its most brilliant (plate 97), and it continued to dazzle in the early part of the century (plate 98) until the outbreak of World War I. In the years since then, although there were brief reappearances and reappreciations as late as the mid-1920s, it has been mostly ridiculed. Recently, however, it has been regaining favor; indeed, Art Nouveau jewelry is today so much in demand that forgeries have begun to appear. Collectors should be wary of imitations—particularly of pieces made entirely of metal, as the originals can easily be recast.

Contemporary enthusiasm has of course not always gone hand in hand with discrimination. At its best, Art Nouveau jewelry is admirable; but one should bear in mind that many mediocre variants were produced and that the idiom itself, with its freedom from traditional limits, is fraught with more perils than most. Utter freedom

97

94.
A tortoiseshell brooch with a lattice-and-flower pattern and a honeycomb border of gold piqué, and a pair of tortoiseshell earrings with gold piqué. Italian, mid-nineteenth century. Cooper-Hewitt Museum: gift of Norvin Hewitt Green (brooch) and gift of Mrs. John Innes Kane from the Estate of and in memory of her sister, Mrs. Samuel W. Bridgham (earrings)

95.
A gold brooch and matching earrings incorporating the Etruscan bulla motif. American, c. 1880. Cooper-Hewitt Museum, gift from the Estate of and in memory of Mrs. Robert B. Noyes

96.
A German view of a type of jewelry being created by Tiffany & Company of New York in the late 1890s. An illustration from R. Rücklin's *Das Schmuckbuch*, published by E. A. Seeman, Leipzig, 1901

97.
A pendant of gold, enamel, stone and pearl, combining the water lily, one of the new floral themes inaugurated by Art Nouveau, with the head of an undine, another favorite motif. French, signed *L. Zorra France 1900*. Museum für Kunst und Gewerbe, Hamburg

98.
A necklace of carved horn, tortoiseshell, brown enamel and brown agate mounted in gold, made by René Lalique in 1903 for the St. Louis World's Fair of 1904. French. Walters Art Gallery, Baltimore

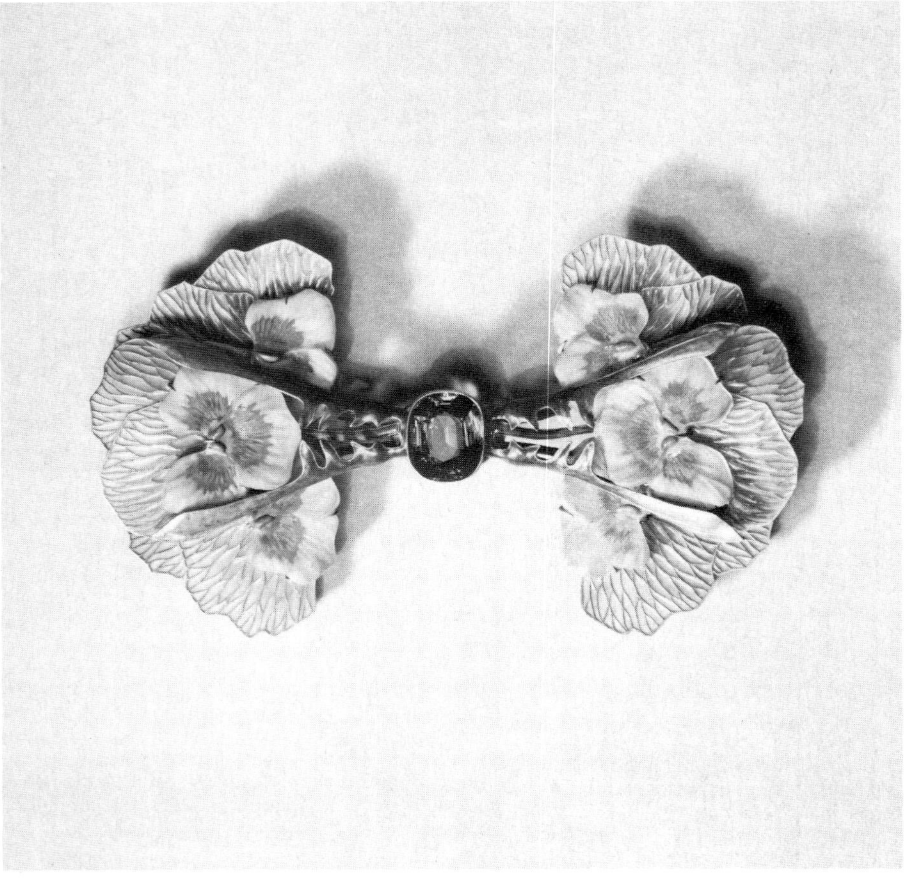

99.
A Lalique pansy brooch, the petals fashioned of molded glass and the stems and leaves of blue enamel; the faceted gem is a step-cut simulated sapphire. French, 1903–4. Walters Art Gallery, Baltimore

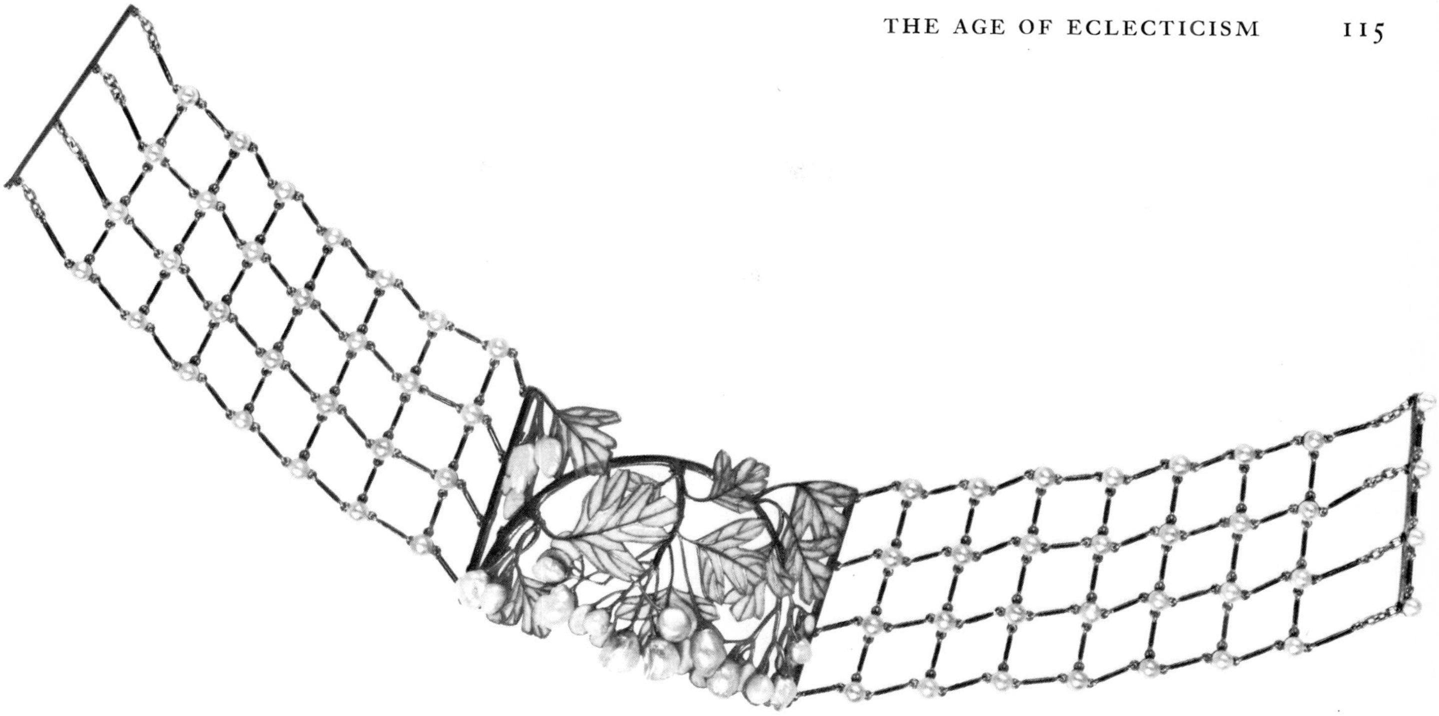

100.
A "dog collar" by René Lalique, of gold, spherical pearls, baroque pearls and plique-à-jour enamel. Signed and dated *Lalique 1900*. Musée des Arts Décoratifs, Paris

101.
A pendant of gold, enamel and diamonds by Henri Vever. The ethereal swan-helmeted maiden seems to have escaped from the pages of one of the great Symbolist writers—Maeterlinck, in all likelihood. Signed and dated *Vever 1900 Paris*. Musée des Arts Décoratifs, Paris

Colorplate 30

Colorplate 31

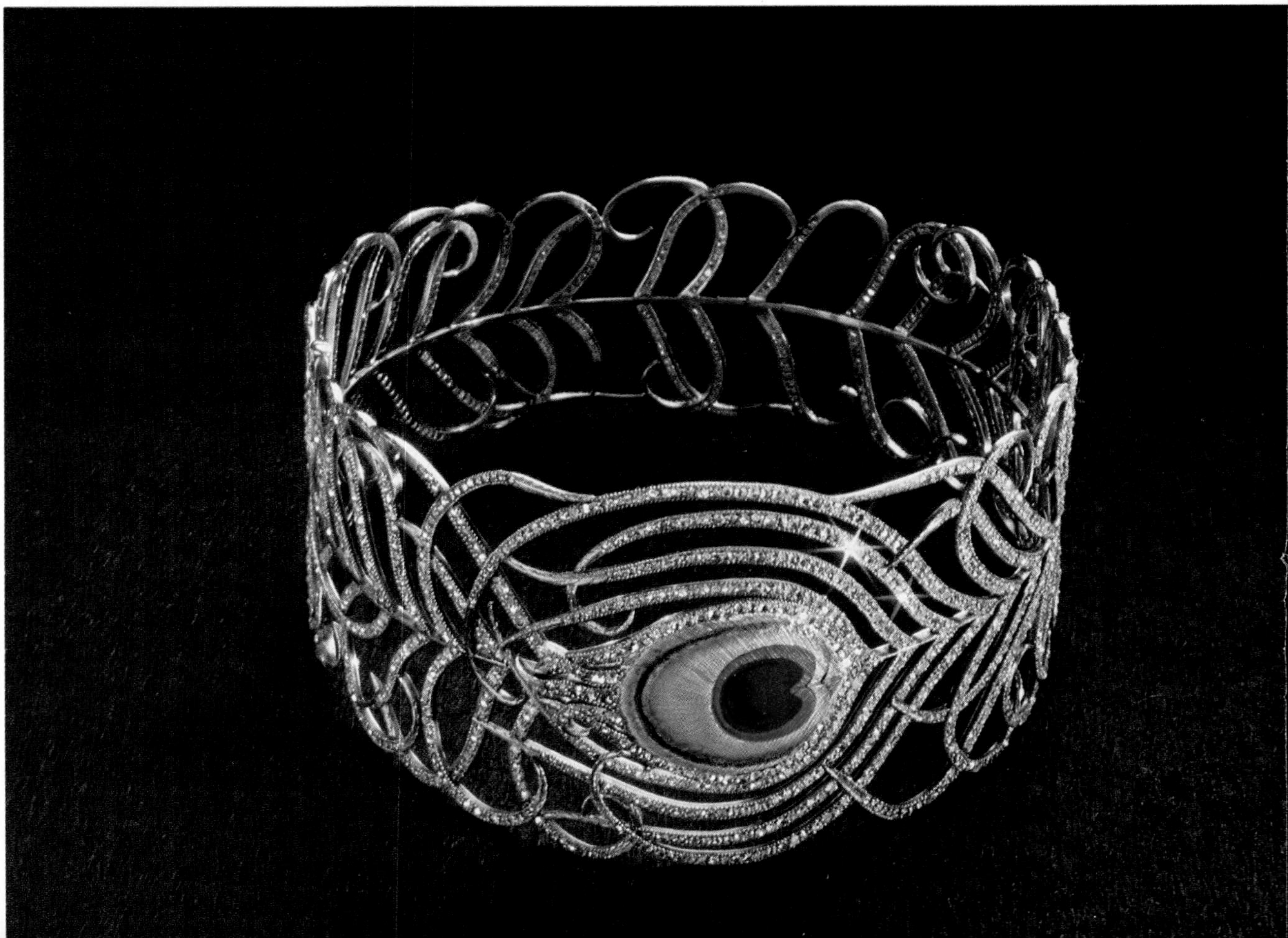

of theme and medium can easily degenerate into tastelessness. A famous element of Art Nouveau design, the "whiplash"—a sinuous, recoiling line of great vitality and expressiveness (colorplate 30)—can, if not firmly controlled by the hand of a master, seem overambitious or even ridiculous.

Happily, Art Nouveau jewelry was dominated from the start by the Frenchman René Lalique (1860–1945), an artist of the first rank by instinct as well as by training (plates 98, 99 and 100). Lalique's versatility and imaginativeness are unmatched. Among his most brilliant rivals were two other French artists, Henri Vever (1854–1942) (plates 101 and 102) and Georges Fouquet (1862–1957), while the Belgian Philippe Wolfers (1858–1929), known as the Flemish Lalique, comes very close indeed.

Many designers of Art Nouveau jewelry were able to carry out their conceptions in precious substances, including diamonds, other gems and the exquisite, frail plique-à-jour enamel—a technique dating back perhaps to twelfth-century France whose revival is attributed principally to Lalique. Some of the most important Art Nouveau objects have extraordinarily beautiful coloring and are veritable jewels for Queen Mab (colorplate 31). There were also Art Nouveau designers who, whether out of principle, like the British jeweler Charles Robert Ashbee (1863–1942), or for practical considerations, limited themselves largely to working in gold or silver, emphasizing purity of form. The style of their jewels is severely sculptural.

A less familiar aspect of Art Nouveau jewelry design involves the work of a number of artists who now appear to deserve special attention as precursors of cubism and Art Deco(ratif). Among them should be mentioned the Scottish craftsman Talwyn Morris (1865–1911), who hammered unique designs at once hypermodern and archaic in gem-encrusted copper and aluminum; and Christian Ferdinand Morawe (b. 1865), a German, whose somewhat barbaric conceptions clearly echo the traditions of African art. Such artists bring us to the end of our course, for we must stop short of the further frontiers of twentieth-century jewelry.

Colorplate 30.
A brass belt buckle with characteristic Art Nouveau features: the opal, pearls and garnets with which it is set and the "whiplash" element of its sculptural design. Probably French, c. 1900. Cooper-Hewitt Museum, gift of Mr. and Mrs. Maxime Hermanos

Colorplate 31.
A gold and diamond "dog collar" in the form of a coiled peacock feather with an enamel eye, this exquisite piece is an early example of the application of the tenets of Art Nouveau to jewelry. From the House of Mellerio (also known as Meller), Paris, c. 1900. Smithsonian Institution, National Collection of Fine Arts, Barney Collection

7 Collecting Antique Jewelry: Pleasures and Pitfalls

The first advice the budding collector of antique jewelry should be given applies to any branch of collecting: learn about your subject by observation and study. Becoming knowledgeable about the stylistic developments and the historical background of jewelry means reading specialized texts; a basic list is given in the bibliography. Catalogues of auction sales and of museum exhibitions are also highly informative, the first as an index of market prices, the second as a gauge of standards. Articles in reviews are also a good source, provided the author is an expert in the field. Because of the glamour of antique jewels and the wealth of historic connotations they frequently carry, magazines of wide readership, however, often publish articles that are stunningly illustrated but otherwise of little value.

Collectors today enjoy an advantage denied their predecessors—excellent illustrations made possible by modern photographic and printing techniques. In many instances, a precise enlargement of the object provides better viewing than a gallery affords, making it *almost* unnecessary to see the original. Almost, but not quite, for familiarity with originals is a must, the only way in which a collector can learn to appreciate such factors as patina, texture and substance.

One practical problem is that jewelry because of its intrinsic preciousness requires careful safekeeping and costly insurance. On the other hand, jewelry requires very little storage space. A fortune in jewels may be carried about in a handbag or stored in a shoe box; the equivalent value of antique furniture would require a moving van.

The would-be collector will have to make one more important decision, and determine how much he can spend in his pursuit. Barring a miracle, it is not realistic to hope to acquire really fine examples of, say, Renaissance jewelry for less than five figures, when they are obtainable at all. Great jewels of any period are extremely

102.
Such an enchantress as Mélusine, Vivien or Mélisande might have inspired this Henri Vever pendant of gold, *pavé* diamonds, rubies, agates and enamel. Signed and dated *Vever Paris 1900*. Musée des Arts Décoratifs, Paris

rare and command great prices. All things being equal, three factors govern the value of an antique jewel: age, rarity and preciousness. But the combinations of the three, in varying proportions, are almost infinite. Where large monetary investments are demanded, the collector should be guided by professional advice. A written guarantee, which reliable merchants will always furnish, should be obtained.

Does this mean that jewelry collecting is ruled out for the person of only "limited" or "modest" means? If punning is allowable, one might answer: by *no* means! A collector whose taste runs to the splendid and costly may learn to enjoy vicarious ownership by collecting not actual jewels but their images. This process, incidentally, is also one of the best ways to build up a background of knowledge prior to actual acquisition, provided the collector keeps proper documentation together with the pictures. Even the most attentive reading is purely passive, while a compilation of carefully documented illustrations involves the "collector" actively and personally.

A second possibility lies in limiting one's area of collecting: a collector may concentrate on a narrow sliver of the entire spectrum. He might, for instance, specialize in such trinkets as the dainty wrist chains that were used during the Victorian era to tighten sleeve ruffles. Because the chains are frequently made of gold or silver, they often pass as bracelets, but in fact they were functional, not ornamental. Because of their frailty—they are hardly more than a metallic woven thread with a delicate small clasp—not many have survived. Yet a patient searcher would find these chains not usually priced out of bounds. In time the collector could bring together an interesting, unusual group of these little-known but charming jewels.

However, it must be admitted that nothing in the field now remains "terra incognita." There are few unexplored areas of jewelry even in the later periods, such as Victorian and Edwardian, including Art Nouveau and the almost contemporary Art Deco. Even the costume jewelry made of celluloid and plastic from the 1920s to the 1950s has been the object of serious interest among collectors.

Fakes and forgeries pose a final problem. Here again a collector's best protection is his familiarity with unquestioned genuine examples, learned through visits to museums and fine shops. Exceptions even to this sound rule occur. For example, the jewelry of the ancient Mediterranean and Near Eastern civilizations has been imitated with skill that deceives even the experts. Renaissance jewelry has also been copied with signal success. Nevertheless, the collector need not be unduly frightened if he keeps in mind that consummate skill of any kind—be it of enameling, as in Renaissance jewelry, or foiling and mounting of glass gems, as in French paste—may be imitated but can never be perfectly duplicated. The forger always falls short in some respect or other, and the trained eye is sensitive to such nuances.

Colorplate 32.
In contrast to the originality and decisiveness of the jewelry of the then-emerging Art Deco movement, the more traditional jewelry of the first quarter of the twentieth century relied primarily for its appeal on preciousness of materials and daintiness of execution. Eclecticism was still the key word: the two examples shown here appear as an epitome of all previous modes and techniques, from Renaissance three-dimensional enameling to eighteenth-century stylization and nineteenth-century realism, all paradoxically combined in the floral motifs.

Left: Pansy brooch-pendant, of gold, diamonds and polychrome enamel. *Right*: Lapel watch, of gold, diamonds and enamel. Both marked *Tiffany & Co.* American, c. 1920. Cooper-Hewitt Museum, gifts of Isabel Shults

Glossary

aglet, a metal tag on a garment, now largely ornamental but originally serving as a fastener or as a device placed at the end of a ribbon or cord to keep it from unraveling.

aigrette, a jeweled ornament, often a spray of gems resembling upright feathers or flowers, worn in the hair or on a hat.

bangle, a rigid bracelet or anklet, often hinged to form two halves.

basse-taille, an enameling technique wherein the metal base to which a translucent enamel will be applied is carved in low relief; it is a refinement of *champlevé.*

bezel, originally the sloping edge that keeps a gem in place in its setting; now applied to the upper face of a finger ring, including any decorative elements, stones or gems and their setting.

bog oak, darkened oak wood found in peat bogs, carved into jewelry during the Victorian era.

briolette, a tear- or pear-shaped gem with overall faceting.

bulla (pl., *bullae*), a globular ornamental motif found in ancient jewelry, thought to have been originated by the Etruscans.

cabochon, a convex, unfaceted but highly polished gem or bead.

cairngorm, yellow or smoky-brown quartz found in the Scottish Highlands.

cameo, a two- or three-layered stone, such as onyx, agate or sardonyx, with ornamentation carved in relief on the generally whitish upper layer, the darker layer or layers beneath serving as a ground. At times cameo-style carving was also done on less precious materials, such as seashell and mother-of-pearl, as well as on artificially layered substances.

cannetille, mountings of very thin gold used in jewelry of the straitened economic period following the fall of the First Empire in France.

carcanet, an ornamental headband, collar, chain or necklace worn until about the seventeenth century.

champlevé, an enameling technique in which the enamel flux is placed in shallow troughs scooped out of a metal base.

chatelaine, originally a practical device worn by women, consisting of a hook or clasp attached to the waistband of a garment and equipped with a number of short chains from which hung needlecase, thimble, scissors, keys and other domestic items; it became more decorative from the seventeenth century on.

chrysocale, a mid-nineteenth-century alloy of copper, pewter and zinc, resembling gold; much used in the manufacture of the cheaper jewelry of the period.

cloisonné, a type of enameling in which the colored enamels are poured into sections, or "cells" (French, *cloisons*), formed by metal partitions set on a metal base.

collet, a sloping metal band that encircles a gem and holds it in place, as a collar encircles the neck; sometimes used interchangeably with *bezel,* although in modern times the latter term has lost this specialized sense.

commesso (pl., *commessi*), a Renaissance jewel with a cameo or other carved stone completed by decorative elements, such as chased gold for the long flowing hair of a woman's head or gem-encrusted gold for a warrior's helmet. *Commessi* continued fitfully in favor until the nineteenth century, when they were revived full force by the jewelry designers of Art Nouveau.

cope morse, see *morse.*

counterpoise, an element hanging at the back of a necklace to balance the weight of the front section and keep it in place.

dog collar, a high, wide band worn tight around the neck, made of strands of beads, gems, pearls and the like, or sometimes of a broad ribbon with rigid metallic elements at intervals to hold it upright; not widely popular until the late nineteenth century, although one Renaissance example is known and in ensuing periods it was prefigured by velvet bands and narrow ribbon and lace ruffs centering a jewel.

en ronde bosse, in high relief; in some instances, three-dimensional, as in figural jewels of the medieval and Renaissance periods.

enseigne, in the Middle Ages, a badge pinned to the hat to signify a pilgrimage to a shrine; later, a decorative medallion usually worn on a hat or a cap.

ferronnière, a slender chain with a jeweled clasp or pendant at the center, worn around the head slightly above the eyes; in favor during the Renaissance, it was revived in the romantic period (about 1830–45).

fibula (pl., *fibulae*), an ancient brooch, functional as well as ornamental; the forerunner of the modern safety pin.

filigree, metallic ornamentation of great delicacy, consisting of wire or beads, or both, in lacy patterns.

foil, a thin metal backing for gems, to supply additional color and brilliance; in ancient times, used for precious stones, including diamonds, as well as for glass; an essential element of *paste.* See also *verre églomisé.*

girandole, a type of earring or brooch created in the seventeenth century, with three tear-shaped pendants suspended from a central ornament.

granulation, a method of decorating a metal surface with minute gold beads or grains.

intaglio, a gem or other stone incised with a sunken pattern; the opposite of a *cameo,* which is carved with a raised pattern.

morse, a very large brooch or clasp, often richly jeweled, used to fasten the front of a cope.

niello, a decorative technique in which a design engraved in a metal base is covered with a black flux and the excess removed so that the black design appears level with the metal ground; essentially a monochromatic version of *champlevé* enameling.

parure, a set of matched jewels, commonly consisting of a necklace, earrings, bracelets and brooches, but oftentimes including a tiara, comb and belt buckle too. Under the First Empire in France, the *grande parure* was the full set, reserved for court wear; the *demiparure* included two or three items, but never the tiara and comb, and was worn on less formal occasions.

paste, French paste or *antique paste* (or *strass*), a fine jewelry of the late eighteenth and early nineteenth centuries, featuring foiled gem-cut glass and generally set in silver.

pavé, a type of setting in which gems or stones are mounted so close together that no metal is visible between them.

pendeloque, a flat, tear-shaped drop. Pendeloque earrings have only one pendant instead of three, as in the *girandole*.

pietra dura (pl., *pietre dure*), mosaic work made with fragments of stone or semi-precious minerals, as distinguished from that made with particles of glass; both kinds are found in jewelry. Such jewelry was particularly popular during the mid-Victorian era.

pinchbeck, an alloy of zinc and copper, brassy gold in color; named for its inventor, the English watchmaker Christopher Pinchbeck (c. 1670–1732).

piqué, the decoration of tortoiseshell with gold or silver inlay.

plique-à-jour, a very delicate enameling technique in which the enamel is suspended on a lattice of slender wiring, with no metal ground below; the effect is of stained glass.

repoussé, decorative work on metal done by hammering or pressing the design on the back, so that it appears in relief on the front; used on jewelry since ancient times.

ruolz, metal resembling gold or silver; named after the French chemist who invented the process whereby it was gilded or silvered.

semé, a heraldic term for a repeat quincuncial pattern.

stomacher, a large and often triangular jeweled ornament worn on the bodice, sometimes extending from the low-cut neckline to the tip of the pointed waist; in fashion during the mid-eighteenth century and revived during the late nineteenth.

strapwork, decorative design based on variations of the band motif; frequently used in late Renaissance jewelry.

strass, a type of *paste*; it was named for Georges-Frédéric Stras, or Strass, who developed it.

table cut, an early style of gem cutting, in which the upper part of the stone was cut straight across, producing a large flat face called the *table*.

tremblant, a type of gem setting in which the stones, usually diamonds, are mounted on hidden springs so that they quiver continually; the result is great lightness and sparkle.

vermeil, gilded silver.

verre églomisé, the ancient technique of painting on the reverse of glass, often with gold or silver foil laid on as a ground, and then sealing in the painted decoration by fusing a second layer of glass to the first; named for Jean-Baptiste Glomy (d. 1786), a Parisian craftsman who adapted and simplified the process to decorate glass picture frames.

verroterie, glass baubles, beads and trinkets, as well as gem-cut glass, used as elements of jewelry.

Reading and Reference

General

BRADFORD, ERNLE. *Four Centuries of European Jewellery*. London: Country Life, 1967.

BRITISH MUSEUM. *Jewellery Through 7000 Years*. London: British Museum Publications, 1976.

BURGESS, FREDERICK W. *Antique Jewelry & Trinkets*. 1919. Reprint. New York: Tudor Publishing Co., 1972.

COOPER UNION MUSEUM. *Italian Drawings for Jewelry, 1700–1875*. New York: Cooper Union Museum, 1940.

DAVENPORT, CYRIL. *Jewellery*. London: Methuen & Co., 1905.

EVANS, JOAN. *English Jewellery from the Fifth Century* A.D. *to 1800*. New York: E. P. Dutton & Co., 1921.

———. *A History of Jewellery, 1100–1870*. 2d ed., rev. and reset. London: Faber & Faber, 1970. Extensive bibliography.

FALKINER, RICHARD. *Investing in Antique Jewelry*. New York: Clarkson N. Potter, 1968.

FONTENAY, EUGÈNE. *Les Bijoux Anciens et Modernes*. Paris, 1887. Excellent illustrations.

GERE, CHARLOTTE. *American & European Jewelry, 1830–1914*. New York: Crown Publishers, 1975.

HORNUNG, CLARENCE P. *A Source Book of Antiques & Jewelry Designs*. New York: George Braziller, 1968.

HUGHES, GRAHAM. *Jewelry*. New York: E. P. Dutton & Co., 1966.

LANLLIER, JEAN, AND MARIE-ANNE PINI. *Cinq Siècles de Joaillerie en Occident*. Fribourg, Switzerland: Office du Livre, 1971. Excellent illustrations.

PERCIVAL, MACIVER. *Chats on Old Jewellery and Trinkets*. New York: Frederick A. Stokes Co., n.d.

ROGERS, FRANCES, AND ALICE BEARD. *5000 Years of Gems & Jewelry*. New York: Frederick A. Stokes Co., 1940.

SMITH, H. CLIFFORD. *Jewellery*. New York: G. P. Putnam's Sons, 1908.

STEINGRÄBER, ERICH. *Antique Jewelry*. New York: Frederick A. Praeger, 1957.

Regalia

BAPST, G. *Histoire des Joyaux de la Couronne de France*. Paris, 1889.

BUNT, CYRIL G. E. "The Medici Crown." *The Connoisseur*, March 1941.

ESTREICHER, KAROL. *The Mystery of the Polish Crown Jewels*. London: Alliance Press, 1945.

TWINING, EDWARD FRANCIS. *A History of the Crown Jewels of Europe*. London: B. T. Batsford, 1960.

———. *European Regalia*. London: B. T. Batsford, 1967.

The Age of Gold

Aldred, Cyril. *Jewels of the Pharaohs: Egyptian Jewelry of the Dynastic Period.* New York: Praeger Publishers, 1971.

Edwards, I. E. S. *Tutankhamun's Jewelry.* New York: Metropolitan Museum of Art, 1976.

Evans, Arthur. *The Palace of Minos at Knossos.* 1936. Reprint. New York: Agathon Press, 1963.

Higgins, R. A. *Greek and Roman Jewellery.* London: Methuen & Co., 1961.

Hoffmann, Herbert, and Patricia F. Davidson. *Greek Gold: Jewelry from the Age of Alexander.* Boston: Museum of Fine Arts, 1965. Exhibition catalogue.

Metropolitan Museum of Art. *Ancient Egyptian Jewelry.* New York: Metropolitan Museum of Art, 1940.

———. "From the Lands of the Scythians." *The Metropolitan Museum of Art Bulletin,* XXXII, no. 5 (1975).

———. *Greek and Etruscan Jewelry: A Picture Book.* New York: Museum Press, 1940.

———. *Thracian Treasures from Bulgaria.* New York: Metropolitan Museum of Art, 1977. Exhibition catalogue.

The Middle Ages and the Renaissance

d'Otrange, M.-L. "A Collection of Renaissance Jewels at the Art Institute of Chicago." *The Connoisseur,* September 1952.

———. "Jewels of the XVth and XVIth Centuries." *The Connoisseur,* November 1953.

d'Otrange Mastai, M.-L. "A Collection of Renaissance Jewels." *The Connoisseur,* April 1957.

———. "Imperial Treasures." *Apollo,* December 1954.

Evans, Joan. *Magical Jewels of the Middle Ages and the Renaissance, Particularly in England.* Oxford: Oxford University Press, 1922.

Hackenbroch, Yvonne. *Renaissance Jewellery.* London: Sotheby Parke Bernet Publishers, 1979.

Lesley, Parker. *Renaissance Jewels and Jeweled Objects in the Melvin Gutman Collection.* Baltimore: Baltimore Museum of Art, 1968.

Metropolitan Museum of Art. *Mediaeval Jewelry: A Picture Book.* New York: Museum Press, 1940.

———. *Renaissance Jewelry: A Picture Book.* New York: Museum Press, 1940.

Ricketson, Edith B. "Barbarian Jewelry of the Merovingian Period." *The Metropolitan Museum of Art Bulletin,* V, no. 5 (1947).

Riefstahl, Rudolf M. "European Jeweled Arts." *Museum News: Toledo [Ohio] Museum of Art,* Autumn 1970.

Rowe, Donald F., S. J. *The Art of Jewelry, 1450–1650.* Chicago: Martin d'Arcy Gallery of Art, Loyola University, 1975. Exhibition catalogue.

The Age of the Diamond

Lewis, M. D. S. "Antique Garnet Jewellery." *The Connoisseur Yearbook,* 1957.

———. *Antique Paste Jewellery.* Boston: Book & Art Publisher, 1970.

Nollet, Jacqueline R. "Eighteenth Century Paste Jewelry." *The Antiquarian,* December 1929.

Oman, Charles. "The Jewels of Our Lady of the Pillar at Saragossa." *Apollo,* June 1967.

Ryley, A. Beresford. *Old Paste.* London: Methuen & Co., 1913.

The Age of Eclecticism

Armstrong, Nancy. *Victorian Jewelry.* New York: Macmillan Publishing Co., 1976.

Bury, Shirley. "Pugin's Marriage Jewellery." *Victoria and Albert Museum Yearbook,* 1969.

Castellani, Alessandro. *Antique Jewellery and Its Revival.* Philadelphia: Pennsylvania Museum and School of Industrial Art, n.d. (c. 1876).

Cooper, Diana, and Norman Battershill. *Victorian Sentimental Jewelry.* Cranbury, N.J.: A. S. Barnes & Co., 1973.

d'Otrange, M.-L. "The Exquisite Art of Carlo Giuliano." *Apollo,* June 1954.

Flower, Margaret. *Victorian Jewelry.* Rev. ed. Cranbury, N.J.: A. S. Barnes & Co., 1973.

Gere, Charlotte. *Victorian Jewelry Design.* Chicago: Henry Regnery Co., 1972.

Janson, Dora Jane. *From Slave to Siren: The Victorian Woman and Her Jewelry, from Neoclassic to Art Nouveau.* Durham, N.C.: Duke University Museum of Art, 1971.

McClinton, Katharine Morrison. *Lalique for Collectors.* New York: Charles Scribner's Sons, 1975.

Mourey, Gabriel, and Aymer Vallance. *Art Nouveau Jewelry & Fans.* New York: Dover Publications, 1973.

Osmun, William R. *Nineteenth Century Jewelry: From the First Empire to the First World War.* New York: Cooper Union Museum, 1955.

Warren, Geoffrey. *All Color Book of Art Nouveau.* New York: Crown Publishers, 1974.

Some Public Collections of Jewelry

UNITED STATES

Baltimore: The Walters Art Gallery
Boston: Museum of Fine Arts
Cleveland: Cleveland Museum of Art
Los Angeles: Los Angeles County Museum of Art
New York City: The Brooklyn Museum
Cooper-Hewitt Museum, the Smithsonian Institution's National Museum of Design
The Metropolitan Museum of Art
Princeton, N.J.: The Art Museum, Princeton University
Richmond: Virginia Museum of Fine Arts
San Francisco: M. H. de Young Memorial Museum
Toledo, Ohio: The Toledo Museum of Art
Washington, D.C.: Smithsonian Institution
National Collection of Fine Arts
National Museum of Natural History

OTHER

Ankara: Archaeological Museum
Athens: Benaki Museum   National Archaeological Museum
Baghdad: Iraq Museum
Berlin: Kunstgewerbemuseum
Budapest: Iparmüvészeti Múzeum (Museum of Applied Arts)
Cairo: Coptic Museum   Egyptian Museum
Dresden: Grünes Gewölbe
Dublin: National Museum of Ireland
Florence: Museo dell'Opificio delle Pietre Dure
Istanbul: Topkapi Sarayi Müzesi
Kiev: Historical Museum
Leningrad: State Hermitage Museum
London: British Museum   Victoria and Albert Museum
Luton, England: Wernher Collection, Luton Hoo
Mainz, West Germany: Mittelrheinisches Landemuseum   Römisch-Germanisches Zentralmuseum
Moscow: Kremlin Museums: State Armory Museum
Munich: Bayerisches Nationalmuseum   Residenzmuseum
Staatliche Antikensammlung und Gyptothek
Palermo: Museo Nazionale
Paris: Bibliothèque Nationale   Musée des Arts Décoratifs
Musée de Cluny   Musée du Louvre
Pforzheim, West Germany: Schmuckmuseum Pforzheim im Reuchlinhaus
Rome: Musei e Gallerie Pontificie
Vienna: Kunsthistoriches Museum   Österreichisches Museum für angewandte Kunst
Zurich: Kunstgewerbemuseum

Index

Numbers in *italics* indicate pages on which black-and-white illustrations appear. Numbers in **boldface** indicate pages on which colorplates appear.

Acknowledgments

Cooper-Hewitt staff members have been responsible for the following contributions to the series: concept, Lisa Taylor; administration, Christian Rohlfing, David McFadden and Kurt Struver; coordination, Peter Scherer. In addition, valuable help has been provided by S. Dillon Ripley, Joseph Bonsignore, Susan Hamilton and Robert W. Mason of the Smithsonian Institution, as well as by the late Warren Lynch, Gloria Norris and Edward E. Fitzgerald of Book-of-the-Month Club, Inc.

Credits

Copyright A.C.L.-Bruxelles: 41, 42. The Ashmolean Museum, Oxford, England: 34. Bayerische Verwaltung der staatlichen Schlösser, Gärten und Seen, Munich: 38, 46; color 23. Bibliothèque Nationale, Paris: 33. Bildarchiv Preussischer Kulturbesitz, West Berlin: 44. Lee Boltin: color 3, 5, 6. Courtesy of the Trustees of the British Museum, London: 6, 52–54. Harry Burton: 2. Cleveland Museum of Art, Cleveland, Ohio: 45, 77. Cliché des Musées Nationaux, Paris: 18, 36, 37, 39. Cooper-Hewitt Museum: 64, 72 and 79 (Scott Hyde); 85 (George D. Cowdery); 75, 80, 82, 84 (left), 86–95 and color *frontispiece*, 24 (lower left), 25–30, 32 (Helga Photo Studio, Inc.). Courtesy of the Dumbarton Oaks Collection, Washington, D.C.: color 9. Permission of The Fine Arts Museums of San Francisco: 28. Gabinetto Fotografico Soprintendenza beni artistici e storici di Firenze: 40, 47, 50. Copyright reserved Galerie Thyssen, Lugano-Castagnola: 51. Germanisches Nationalmuseum, Nuremberg: 1. Giraudon, Paris: 32. Los Angeles County Museum of Art, Los Angeles, Cal.: 14. The Metropolitan Museum of Art, New York: 3–5, 13, 17, 19–21, 25, 27, 31, 49, 55, 56, 59–61, 70, 74, 81, 83; color 2, 4, 8, 10 (Malcolm Varon), 11, 12 (Malcolm Varon), 13, 16–20. Günter Meyer, Copyright Foto-Werbestudio, Pforzheim, West Germany: 15. Photo Meyer K.G., Vienna: color 14 (left). Copyright © Museo del Prado, Madrid: 69. Museum für Kunst und Gewerbe, Hamburg: 97. Courtesy Museum of Fine Arts, Boston: 9. Courtesy of the Trustees, The National Gallery, London: 67. National Gallery of Art, Washington, D.C.: 48, 62; color 14 (right), 15. National Museum of Ireland, Dublin: 35. National Portrait Gallery, London: 73. © 1979 Trustees of Princeton University, Princeton, N.J.: 11. Private collection: 76, 78, 84 (right) and color 24 (except lower left) by Helga Photo Studio, Inc.; 96 by Scott Hyde. Tom Scott, Edinburgh: 43. Seattle Art Museum, Seattle, Wash.: 8. Smithsonian Institution, Washington, D.C.: 22, 58 and color, 21, 31 (National Collection of Fine Arts); color 1 (National Museum of Natural History). Photo Laurent Sully, Jaulmes, Paris: 65. The Toledo Museum of Art, Toledo, Ohio: 57. Union Centrale des Arts Décoratifs, Paris: 100–102. Victoria and Albert Museum, London, Crown Copyright: 71. Virginia Museum of Fine Arts, Richmond: 10, 16. The Walker Art Gallery, Liverpool: 66 (John Mills Photography). Courtesy of The Walters Art Gallery, Baltimore: 24, 26, 29, 30, 63, 68, 98, 99; color 7, 22.

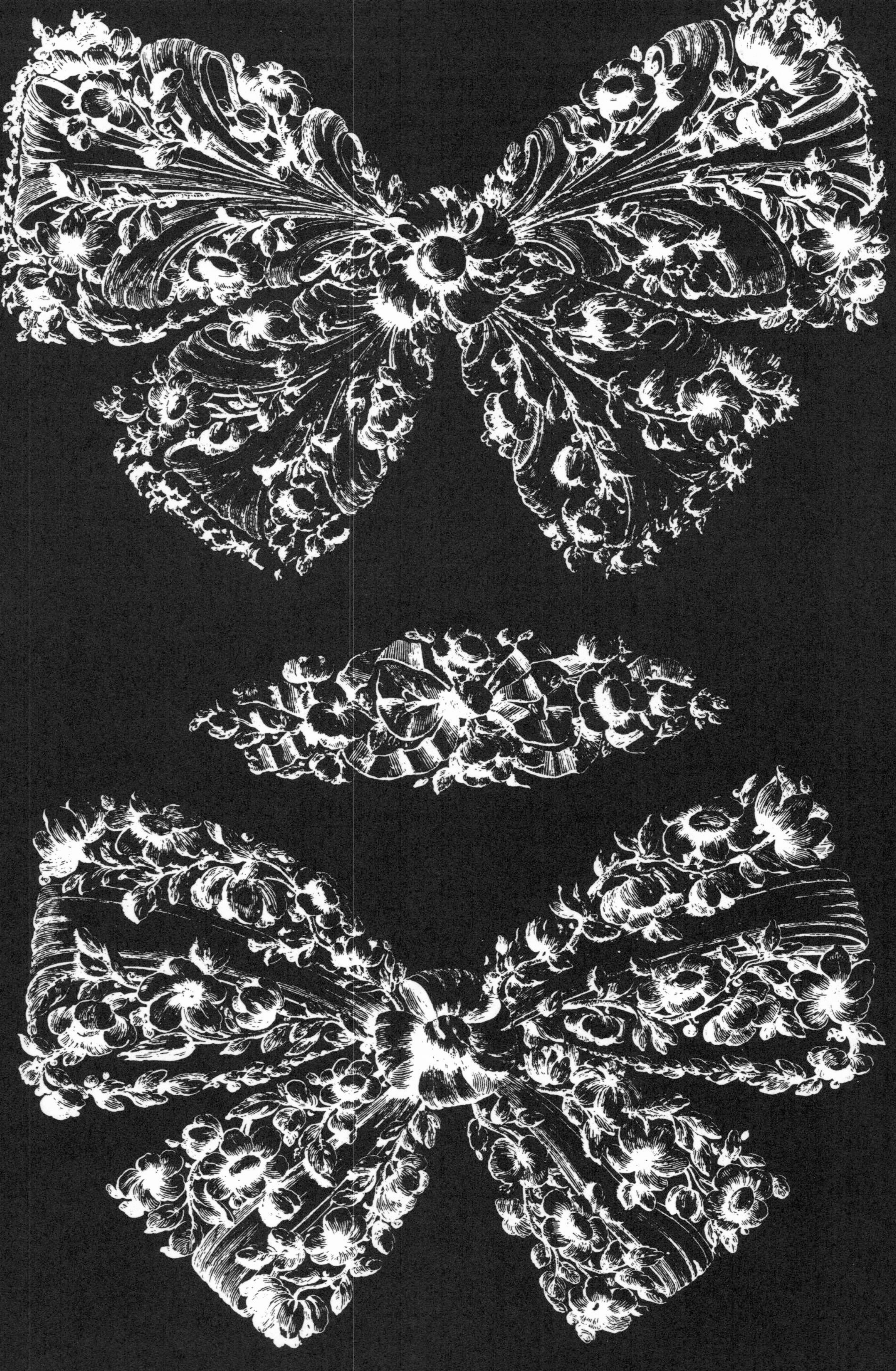